12/25/85

merry Christmas Papa
Love,
Mark, Jeff + K

DEAR PETE The Life Of PETE ROSE

by

Helen Fabbri

Edited by

Larry D. Names

Laranmark Press

BookWrights, Inc.   *Neshkoro, Wisconsin*

Published by Laranmark Press

220 Main Street
Neshkoro, Wisconsin 54960

ISBN: 0-910937-36-2

Box 253
Neshkoro, WI 54960

First Printing September 1985

Printed by
Bookcrafters
Chelsea, Michigan

Table of Contents

Bibliography

The following is a list of all the source materials used by the author and editing staff for the preparation of this book. Many of the quotes attributed to Pete Rose in this book were related to the author by him, and as many of the other quotes are duplicated in more than one publication, footnoting each quote to its original printed source is impractical:

The Pete Rose Story, An Autobiography; Pete Rose; The World Publishing Co.; 1970

Charlie Hustle; Pete Rose with Bob Hertzel; Prentice-Hall, Inc.; 1975

Rose show hits town; Hubert Mizell; St. Petersburg Times; 1979

Climbing High on Baseball's Hit List; Jayson Stark; Baseball, Street & Smith's Official Yearbook; Conde Nast Publications, Inc.; 1982

The Baseball Encyclopedia, Sixth Edition; Joseph L. Reichler; MacMillan Publishing Co.; 1985

4192!; United Press International; Contemporary Books, Inc.; 1985

On Deck For The Big Knock; Rick Reilly; Sports Illustrated; August 19, 1985

Cutting A Hit Record; Craig Neff; Sports Illustrated; Sept. 16, 1985

The Record and Rose; Paul Attner; The Sporting News; Sept. 16, 1985

The World Almanac & Book of Facts; Newspaper Enterprise Association; 1972, 1974, 1978, 1984, 1985

The World Book Encyclopedia Year Book; Field Enterprises Educational Corporation; 1971, 1972, 1973, 1974, 1975, 1976, 1977, 1978, 1979, 1980

Baseball, Street & Smith's Official Yearbook; Conde Nast Publications, Inc.; 1981, 1982, 1983, 1984, 1985

FOREWORD

Over the years I received hundreds of thousands of letters from my fans. This collection of letters contains samples of their feelings, both toward me and the sport of baseball. It is the fans that make baseball the fun and exciting sport that it is. These fan letters illustrate your love for the game and the players who participate in it.

I particularly enjoy letters from the many young people who write. Their innocence and faith in me makes all the hard work and effort worthwhile. With Helen's help, I tried to answer each and every one of them.

I hope you enjoy the letters as much as I do. Although some are not complimentary, they do provide an insight into what the public feels and thinks about America's number one pastime.

Helen has been my fan mail secretary for many years and her book brings back many fond memories. I want to thank her for the tireless help she has given me and her dedication to the sport of baseball. Since this book is the only authorized collection of my fan letters, I wish her all the success in the world.

Pete Rose

ACKNOWLEDGEMENTS

Several people have provided advice and, more importantly, help with the production of this book. They have contributed to my attempt to achieve the quality that the subject of this book, Pete Rose, deserves.

First and foremost, I thank my husband Tony for his help. He ran a lot of errands for me, made photocopies of everything, and made dozens of trips to the post office.

Then there's my son Tony, Jr., and my lovely daughter-in-law Wanda. Wanda edited my manuscript before any publisher ever saw it, and Tony, Jr., made extra copies of everything for me.

My daughters Joyce and Janice helped me select the letters for this book and did the typing. I don't know how I would have done it without her help.

And all the people who took my raw manuscript and made it into a book, I thank them, too. Greg Scott and John Torinus for their editorial advice; Peggy Eagan for creating such a beautiful cover; John Braude of the Cincinnati Reds Public Relations Department for supplying the cover photo of Pete; Donna Shankleton for believing in this book; and my editor, for his invaluable professional assistance, Larry Names.

And, of course, Pete Rose, for giving me permission to write this book about him and for the use of his mail.

To Tony, my husband, who helped with the mail and had so much patience with me while I was writing; and to my grandsons, Troy, Tony Gene, and Brett, in the hope that they pursue their dreams with as much enthusiasm as Pete has on his race to the big one, #4,192!

And to the memory of
Harry "Pete" Rose
for instilling in his son
the discipline of hustle.

Hustle past, present, future: the Rose men.
Harry, Pete, Petey, and Ty.

1

Never Let Down

Hustle! Hear it? *Hustle!* See it? *Hustle!* Feel it? *Hustle!*

And what comes to mind?

There's only one answer: Pete Rose.

From the day his name made the lineup card for the human race, Pete Rose has been hustling, on the move, always straight ahead. But why? And for what goal?

Roy Hobbs, the character Robert Redford portrayed in the 1984 hit film *The Natural*, said, "I want to walk down the street and have people point at me and say, 'There goes Roy Hobbs, the best there ever was.'"

Pete Rose wants people to point at him and say, "There's Pete Rose who was the best he could be."

Peter Edward Rose was born April 14, 1941 — the year after Boston changed its name from the Bees back to the Braves, the hit song was *Hut-Sut Rawlson*, the Japanese bombed Pearl Harbor, England had "it's finest hour" in the air war with Germany, the Reds under Bill McKechnie had finished third, and Detroit's Hank Greenberg belted out two home runs to beat the New York Yankees, 7 to 4, only to be drafted into the army the next day. The year after Joe DiMaggio had ended a fifty-six game batting streak when he went hitless against the Cleveland Indians. They say when Joe ended his streak, he sighed and said, "I'm tickled to death it's over."

Right off he was called "Little Pete" by his mom, LaVerne, because his dad, whose real name was Harry, was already known as Pete Rose. Harry Rose acquired the nickname as a child because of his affection for a vegetable cart horse named Pete. Outside of the family father and son were known as Pete and Re-Pete because it seemed that everywhere "Big" Pete went "Little Pete" was right behind.

Harry Rose was one proud father; he had a son. And "Little Pete" had a father he'll always be proud of. Harry was one of the best athletes Cincinnati has ever known. He had been an amateur boxer, weighing in at 105 pounds, winning a state amateur crown for special weight class, and serving as a sparring partner for former world featherweight champion Freddie Miller. He was also a pretty fair baseball player, and a halfback and defensive back with the original Cincinnati Bengals football team. "Big" Pete played organized football until he was 42, and some of his gridiron feats are still legendary in the Ohio Valley.

Like all fathers Harry had hopes and dreams for his son. But instead of just hoping and dreaming, he helped his son in every way he could. He did the best thing any father could: he set a good example. He didn't drink hard liquor; he didn't smoke; and he didn't fight with "Little Pete's" mother. He worked hard at whatever he did, whether it was playing football or carrying out his daily duties as a bank employee. And it wasn't just for "Little Pete's" benefit. Harry Rose was that way — all the time.

Every boy grows up with dreams of his own, but not every boy's dreams come true. Pete Rose grew up dreaming he could make his father's dreams come true.

"Little Pete" was raised on a steady diet of baseball, baseball, baseball! Cincinnati Reds baseball. Knot Hole League baseball. Sandlot baseball. Even "house ball", a game he played with his younger brother Dave whenever he was stuck close to home. He attended almost every game the Cincinnati Reds played or so it seemed. When he wasn't at Crosley Field in person, he sat at home listening to every word of play-by-play coverage on the radio. And when he wasn't into the Reds games in person or over the airwaves, he was *playing* them with his active imagination, an aspect that drove his teachers crazy every spring.

Pete and Dave played "house ball" morning, noon, and as far into the night as their mother would permit by bouncing a rubber ball off a red-brick wall at Schulte's, a fish place near their home in Anderson Ferry, a section of western Cincinnati. Pete recollected that they played so much "house ball" against that old red-brick building that they must have worn the paint away so fast that every six months or so the building would have to be repainted.

When he wasn't playing "house ball", Pete collected empty pop bottles and cashed them in for spending money. Or he rode the ferryboat, *Boone Number Seven*, a rickety side-wheeler that ran back and forth between Ohio and Kentucky. Or he and some guys his age would climb up the steep Ohio hillside, overlooking their river valley community, sometimes camping there all night. In the morning they'd eat bacon cooked by campfire and watch the river mist evaporate to let the Kentucky hills — across the river — come back from whatever place the fog had hidden them. Or they'd play along the river bank itself at the ferry landing. But most of the time, Pete would be in Schulte's parking lot, dodging customers while he played "house ball", and he'd be pretending he was with the Cincinnati Reds.

A boyhood dream! And it all came true! And how it came true!

Anderson Ferry is one of the older towns along the Ohio River, just a few miles west of downtown Cincinnati. The community is locked in the narrow valley. Indians would cross the river there long before the first ferry began. Legend has it that during the Civil War this was the place Morgan's Raiders entered Ohio to rampage through the countryside. The Ohio River valley at Anderson Ferry was only two streets wide when Pete was growing up. Then it ends abruptly, blocked by a steep hill. Railroad trains — the Baltimore and Ohio as well as the Penn Central — whistle west through this bottle-neck valley on their way west. The valley is grimy and noisy and fun. Anderson Ferry is known mostly for the ferry, Schulte's where people came from all over to eat the lake trout, and — later — the Trolley Tavern and the Flying Bridge, two restaurants known for their atmospheres, each having a mixture of streetcar and riverboat motifs.

Pete has told the story of how he and friends, when going on one of their camping trips, would stop first at Schulte's, where Henry Lapp and Ken Rudusell, both of whom worked at the fish restaurant, would give them French fries for the outing. On nights when they were supposed to be camping but didn't really feel like going, they would ride the "owl bus" to the end of the line at Saylor Park and back again up into the city — the whole night.

In a reflective mood once, Pete asked the rhetorical question, "I wonder what makes the remembering of childhood, though, seem so sad?" Then he answered himself with, "I mean, it's like thinking back and re-membering a baseball team that has been scattered nine different ways and isn't any more."

Pete has lots of memories of his youth — some sad, but most happy. He recalled the time the Trolley Tavern caught fire and George Wells was up on the roof of the restaurant, chopping holes in it. Then when the Texaco river terminal caught fire, the fire hoses, strung across the railroad track, were okay till a freight train came through and every hose was cut. That memory is particularly vivid in Pete's mind because he was playing baseball when the first gasoline tank exploded. And there was the awful night a drunken man was killed by a train.

But above all, Pete remembers baseball "because

baseball was all that mattered to me." Backyard baseball with his sisters, Jackie and Caryle, and his cousin
Lois; sandlot ball; playing on various teams at different
age levels; Pete, always with a baseball glove hooked to
his belt. He described Jackie as "a pretty sharp little
ballplayer." Come his ninth summer, he graduated
from the red-brick wall at Schulte's to his first for-real
baseball team: the Sedamsville Civic Club. He was the
catcher, and the team played at Bold Face Park in
Sedamsville, which was close to the Penn Central
freight yards and the Ohio River.

Helping Pete to realize his dreams, besides his
parents, was his uncle, Ed "Buddy" Bloebaum, his
mother's brother and a great athlete in his own right.
Between them, they took the rough gem every youngster is, nipped a rough edge here and there, polished a
side or two where needed, and gave the world not only
one of the all-time great baseball players, but also gave
the world a sparkling jewel to shine for every youth who
needs a real-life hero. This fact is evidenced by the way
Pete describes his mother and father.

"My mother can get along with anybody. She's that
wonderful. If you can't get along with her, face it, you
just can't get along. She is a wonderful mother. Now
she's an even more wonderful grandmother. When God
made her, He broke the mold.

"My dad? He was about the most important guy in
my life. Right across from the Trolley Tavern was the
Trolley Tavern football field. In the winter my dad
played football there. In the summer my dad played
baseball there. He was a heck of an athlete. A lot of

people will argue with you all day that my dad was the best football player Cincinnati ever had. My dad played football till he was forty-two years old. My mother used to kid him and say that if he didn't quit football, she was going to leave him."

She never did.

Another of Pete's fond childhood memories is when he was the water boy for his father's football team. On Sunday afternoons in the fall, Pete would be sitting at his dad's elbow at the Trolley Tavern — it was known as the Twin Trolleys back then and Pete's mom worked there — listening to the senior Rose and his teammates. Pete related how he could still hear his father hammering one vital principle into him: "If you don't win, Pete, you haven't accomplished anything." Pete claims that any hustle he has in him was inherited from his dad whom he called the "King of Hustle".

Although Harry Rose wasn't a drinking man or a smoker, he did occasionally enjoy a cigar, mostly by chewing them to death. Pete's mother doesn't drink either. As Pete put it, "Our family didn't need booze to get high. We had each other. There was always a lot of exuberance going, and who needs booze?"

Pete admits that once as a kid he did get drunk; it happened after one of his father's football games. They were in Kentucky at a little neighborhood tavern, and the losing team bought a half barrel of beer. Pete decided he could handle it, so he sneaked some brew. Needless to say, he was a very sick young man before the day was through. Throwing up in two states on the same afternoon taught him a valuable lesson. "After that I was more than willing to stick with the milk my mother gave us at our meals. Or when I was daring and wanted to act grown-up, I used to drink a lot of tea."

Pete makes a *semi-lament* that his father was a little strict with him. But for good reason! Harry Rose had a great childhood to Pete's way of thinking because he did so many daring things; such as hop freight trains and ride them into Indiana, jump off and ride another one back home all on the same morning; or Harry and his friends would swim naked in the Ohio River, all the way out to the middle. These were things Harry refused to let Pete do. And Pete knew why. And he loved his father all the more for it.

That was one side of Harry Rose. There was another, softer side that Pete still loves. He tells the story that completely illustrates this other part of his father's character:

"Once when I was little he went downtown to a shoe store with just enough money to buy my sister a pair of shoes. But he never bought those shoes. He saw a pair of miniature boxing gloves — kids size — in a store window. He bought them for me. But when he got home from town and said what he had done, you should have seen the look on my mother's face.

" 'I'm glad about one thing,' my dad said, recalling the look on my mother's face. 'I'm glad they were miniature gloves. If those boxing gloves had been regulation size I think your mother would have put them on herself and given me a real going-over.' "

Harry Rose had an admirable streak of modesty in him. During an interview once, he claimed, "I really was never much of a baseball player. Oh sure, I loved the game when I was younger, but Pete is the *natural-born* baseball player in this family. His ability doesn't come from me. It comes from his mother's side of the family. My brother-in-law Ed (Buddy) Bloebaum is just about the greatest there ever was. When he got his first chance to turn pro he was playing with guys lots older than he was in the K. I. O. League. He even played on the New Arrow team that won the league championship in 1920. He happens to be one of those guys who can do anything on the field and look good while he's doing it. When they first offered him a shot at the big time, he wouldn't consider it. Right then he was managing a pool hall at Fifth and Elm here in Cincinnati. Later on, though, he did go out and play a year at Cedar Rapids."

From his father and uncle, Pete received his elementary education in baseball. He credits them with making a player out of him.

Pete proved himself something of a philosopher, although he'll never admit it, when he pondered a certain point once. He commented on how he spent many spring afternoons in high school staring out the windows dreaming about sports. Then he got "heavy" as the saying goes now:

"That makes sense, though. The dream of my dad was sports, too. Why is it some dads have to pass along their dreams, unrealized, to their kids? What I mean is, except for playing his heart out whenever he played, the only thing my dad has to show for *his* dream is a dumb kid like me who hustles on walks the way some batters hustle on singles. The trouble is, my dad never had the time for sports that I had. He went to old Woodward High School in downtown Cincinnati. Every night after school and every Saturday, too, he worked as a delivery boy for a paper company. He hit the books a lot harder than I ever did. His teachers had convinced him — and rightly so, he said — that if he failed high school he would be a bum for the rest of his life. So between working and hitting the books, my dad never even got to *see* a high school football game all the time he was going to school. Sad, isn't it?

"That's one reason I've got to keep hustling, don't you see? I've got to give my dad, through me, all the moments he never had time for when he, himself, was a kid. If I didn't hustle out there every minute, I'd be letting him down something awful."

The viewer of the movie *Fear Strikes Out*, the story of another baseball great, Jimmy Piersall, was given the impression that Piersall was forced into playing baseball against his will. That could be all Hollywood stuff or the screenplay writer and the director could have gotten that idea, then transferred it to film, from Piersall's book of the same title. Only Jimmy Piersall can answer that question.

But when you read Pete's own words and hear him talk about his father and mother and his uncle and his childhood, the bitterness that seemed to be in Piersall isn't there. If fact, just the opposite is true.

Pete wrote about some of the lessons his father gave him, not all of which pertained to baseball.

"He'd work and work at me, making me bat left-handed. There he'd stand twenty feet away and say,

'Never take your eyes off the ball, Pete. Keep your eye on the ball, Pete. Any time you're doing anything in baseball, keep your eye on the ball.' Before pitching one at me he'd stand there, for as long as three or four minutes, moving the ball this way and that. And, during that time, if he ever caught me not watching the ball, he'd say, 'Okay, Pete, you're not looking.' "

Pete made a habit of keeping his eye on the ball. Watch him when he's batting. He'll watch that ball straight into the catchers glove. He learned that from his dad.

He learned other things, too, like using his left hand more. Harry Rose would say, "Listen, Pete, whenever you're out in the court practicing with a basketball, throw the ball with your left hand. Don't worry about your right hand. Your right hand will develop naturally." Pete is still following that advice.

As aforementioned, Pete began playing on an organized team at the age of nine, and he started as a catcher. He splits the blame or credit between his father and uncle for that. The way Pete tells it, he wasn't too thrilled about being a catcher at first. But looking back now, he's of a different opinion. "I think every kid going into baseball today should have the privilege — and it *is* a privilege — of spending at least one season behind the plate. Being a catcher matures you mentally and physically — fast." Harry and Uncle Buddy didn't have to threaten Pete into playing the position. They merely explained to him why he should, and he accepted their view. They also made a switch-hitter out of Pete.

"I can still remember," Pete said, "standing off to one side, wishing I was somewhere else, as my dad said to the coach, 'I realize that you might run into a championship game, facing a right-handed pitcher. But I want Pete to bat left-handed against every right-hander, no matter what. I want your word that if you want Pete to play for you, he's got to be a switcher.'

"After a long silence during which a freight train whistled in the Riverside yards and started off, with wild huffing and puffing, to Indianapolis, the coach said, 'Okay, fine. You got yourself a deal.' "

The pattern, that long-ago afternoon, was formed.

When recalling that first year of baseball at Bold Face Park, Pete didn't remark on any of his own achievements that year. But what he did relate seems to be of more importance.

"I do remember that when I started my first game, my dad gave up participating in sports for keeps. No more Sunday football with guys half his age. No more playing softball with the guys. 'You're the athlete,' he said. 'Now I can watch you.' I do remember, also, that at the end of the season we got jackets because we were consolation champions or something. Those jackets were beauties. I know because I wanted to sleep in mine. I wore it everywhere. That's how much I loved it. And I do remember, every game he could attend, there would stand my dad, watching every move I made, and I made some pretty dumb ones. I could read his lips clear across the field and they always said the same thing, over and over and over, 'Hustle, Pete. Keep up the hustle.' "

There was one other moment that Pete remembered about that first year of organized play, and it concerned his grandfather.

"And there's one special moment I remember. It concerns my grandfather. He lived in Sedamsville, always played solitaire, and was forever telling me about the time he hit a baseball so hard that it sailed clear out of Bold Face Park, cleared the railroad yards, and landed on the river where it hit a sternwheel steamboat, causing the boat to sink. Only he was dying from cancer all the time I knew him. The day our Knot Hole team played the championship game at Bold Face Park, he insisted that my dad help him out of bed, down the stairs, and across the street to the park so he could see me play. I can still see him, standing on the sidelines, my dad supporting him, and he was shielding his eyes against the sun, watching. I'm glad we won that game. I'm glad we won for the sake of the team and for another — more personal — reason. I loved that old man, shielding his eyes, watching me play. I didn't know that would be the last time he would ever be out of bed. I didn't know that after the game he would go home to die.

"When he died, a part of childhood — for me — seemed over.

"And Bold Face Park — to me — was never the same again."

2

Dear Pete, Send me . . .

"Pete Rose!"

"Hey, Charlie Hustle!"

"Come here!"

"Please come here!"

Go to any ballpark where Pete is playing, and the kids are calling to him. Did I say kids? Teenagers, young adults, middle-aged people, all stand there with pen and program, waiting for an autograph. Some will have baseballs, gloves, and even slips of paper, anything that can be signed.

Pete is a man dedicated to his trade, and he loves every minute of it. "It's fun!" he says. He always runs to first base, and never walks. I don't think he knows what the word *walk* means. From the first game of the season to the last, he gives it his all. He loves what he is doing, and that's the secret ingredient that makes baseball such a great game when he's playing.

Imagine, a game with eighteen men so dedicated. Ah, what a sight to behold!

You are probably wondering how I got such a neat job as Pete Rose's Fan Mail Secretary.

My husband Tony and I had followed the Cincinnati Reds for many years, going to as many games as we could. In late 1974 we decided to get two season tickets to the Cincinnati Red's games. We knew that other members of our family would be able to go to the games if my husband and I couldn't. Since we live about 165 miles from Cincinnati, we decided to rent a furnished apartment for six months. We used it when the Reds were playing home games. Soon, we became hooked on baseball. We then flew to other parks to see the Reds: Pittsburgh, Atlanta, Philadelphia, Los Angeles, San Diego, and San Francisco. On occasion we would drive to Chicago or St. Louis. We always stayed in the same hotel as the players, talking to them and getting to know them. The players were all super. But Pete? He was special.

Many times we would return home from a trip, unpack the suitcases, wash clothes, repack, and head back to Cincinnati, all in a matter of hours.

In 1977 we sold our business, and that left Tony and I with a lot of free time. One day I asked Pete if anyone was taking care of his fan mail. He replied, "No, I never thought of it." I explained about our free time and that I would love to do it. He then replied, "We'll see," as he ran toward his car.

About a week after my talk with Pete, I received a long distance telephone call from Gary Waits, a catcher who warmed up the pitchers in the Reds' bullpen. He said that he had something for me and to stop by the clubhouse after the next home game. When we showed up, what a surprise we got! Pete gave me three large bags of fan mail, stacks of pictures and instructions on what he wanted done. Me, Helen Fabbri from Brazil, Indiana, Pete Rose's Fan Mail Secretary! Wow! Oh, wow! Excited? Who? Me?

I started reading the letters as soon as I got back to the apartment. I could really relate to all the kids who wrote to Pete requesting an autograph, since I have five children of my own. After reading numerous letters, I soon realized that baseball fans are not just kids, but all people, from all walks of life. The game is really universal and touches all age groups.

Nine out of ten letters are from children. Some are very simple: "Pete, please send me your autograph or a picture." Others wanted a baseball signed, a hat, jersey, baseball cards, gloves, posters; you name it, they wanted Pete to send it. Some sent five or ten index cards, wanting each one signed. Not all fan letters were for autographs. Some of the letters that he received are in this book, too precious to discard. The letters are just as I received them, some with incorrect spelling. I deleted the last name of the sender, so as not to embarrass anyone.

I did Pete's mail from 1977 to 1980 when Pete was with the Cincinnati Reds the first time. It was easy to get the mail. Tony and I would go down to the clubhouse after the ballgames, and Pete would bring out the mail to us. About once a month we would visit his home and pick up the mail sent to his home address. When he signed with Philadelphia, the Phillies' home office arranged to have Pete's fan mail answered there. However, I continued to do all the mail that came to Cincinnati. When he went to Canada in 1984 to play for the Montreal Expos, I did his mail during spring training, and the Expos' office took care of his mail until he was traded back to the Reds in August and became their player-manager. Now once again I'm his full-time Fan Mail Secretary.

Dear Mr. Rose,

Could you please send me an autographed picture of you for my ten year old little sister. I want to git it to her for Christmas. Her name is Angela and she says she'd rather play first base for the Cinncinnati Reds than be Miss America. I would really appreciate it.

Thank you,
Linda

What a lovely Christmas surprise! Pete's autographed picture, especially if he is your favorite baseball player!

I am wondering when Angela reaches eighteen if she will still want to be a Cincinnati first baseman. Somehow I think she will change her mind, for being Miss America is the dream of most teenage girls. Time will tell.

Dear Pete Rose,

I am a great fan of yours I like the way you slide. I also like you the best of all the Reds. If I keep on naming all the things I like about you it will take me at least five hundred sheets of

*paper to write it all. To me you and your team are the greatest
in the world. Please send me a autograph picture of yourself.
The bigger the better and put to Mark on the back. I am only ten
years old.*

   love
   Mark

This young gentleman and I will certainly have to
compare our notes on why we like Pete. I know I could
fill quite a few pages myself.

Dear Mr. Rose,
   *I have been to three of your games I think you are super I
think you are the best. One time I almost caught one of your fly
balls. If I would have caught it, it would have burned my hand
off. By the way, could you send me an autograph picture of you
because I'm one of your biggest fans.*

   Sincerely yours
   Scott

The fly ball, when caught, has the hand stinging for a
very long time. Lucky are the fans who bring gloves to
catch them with. When a fly ball makes contact with the
body, such as an arm, you can count on about ten days
of soreness and discoloration.

Dear Pete,
   *Ive alwased admired youre hustle. It seems that everything
you do I do. I cetch and play almost play every position, except
first base. I play left field sometimes and last year I played third
base toward the end of the season. I played I guess pretty good*

to. I played third in the allstars and a few regular games. Tell Johny to Keep up the good work to. Tell him I asked him for the audograph and if he can remember me. I sent you a letter about 2 years ago and forgot to ask you for your audograph. I would like your audograph to. I'm aming to be better than you so keep your eyes open for me in about 7-8 or 9 years. I'm 11 and I want you to just keep playing the way you are. Well good luck this year. I can't write worth a darn either.

   By
   Sincerely,
    Mike

Lets hope the scouts for Redsland observe your playing ability and sign you up in about 9 years. One word of warning, it will take a lot of dedication and hustle to beat "Charlie Hustle's" record.

Dear Pete Rose,
   I have never been to a game of yours because we have 11 people in our family and we really can't afford to but I havn't missed any of the games on T.V. for about 4 or 5 years. I'm 13 and the 7th oldest of the family I have 5 sisters and 3 brothers and of course my parents. I'm in the 7th grade. Special Education at Junior High. I have a disease called cerebal palsey I was born with it and I have a crippled arm and leg but through 3 big operations they have almost fixed my leg but there is nothing they can do for my arm. I would very much appreciate it if you could send me a picture of you and the team autograph. You are my favorite baseball player of all baseball. My dad plays softball and has for 25 years. I have to go I hope I haven't wasted your time.

Thank you very much,
   Roger
P.S. My sister wrote this for me.

I am so glad you wrote such a nice letter to Pete. He always enjoys hearing from his fans. We both hope all the operations prove to be successful. Thank you for writing.

Dear Pete Rose:
   As we sit here watching you play the New York Yankees we can't help but admire you and all your team mates. I wanted to write to you last year and congratulate you buy never got around to it. We watch every televised game that your club plays becuase we really like your style and also we knew "Sparky" when he was with our Front Maple Leafs and always thought the world of hem.
   Pete I'd like to ask a favor of you. Do you have a picture of yourself I can put in our album with Sparky. If there is any charge I will gladly pay for it as I know you must get a lot of requests and pictures do cost money.
   Much good luck Pete to you and your team mates also to you and your lovely wife, please say "hi" to Sparky for us.
   God Bless and Keep up the good work
   Sincerely,
   Mr. and Mrs. W.

Pete and Sparky are the best of friends. I know Pete will be proud to share a space next to his manager "Sparky" in your album.

Dear Mr. Rose,

I watch you on T. V. I saw you on the World Series when you playd the Yankees. And you only had to play four games because you were to good for them. I see you dive into third base how do you do that when I try it I hert my belly and my baseball shirt gets dirty. And how do you cetch so good. I play third base and I always miss and would send me a Pitcher of you!!!

Your base ball fan, I 'm eight years old.

Barry

I never asked Pete if it hurts when he does his famous head first slide, but I'm sure sliding at that speed, it's sure to sting a little. One thing I am certain of, it hurts to observe it, and I'm not the one doing the sliding.

Following is a letter from a small boy who likes Pete. He is just six years old.

Hi Pete Rose,

I am happy that you won the World Series. I saw the last game I hope you are feeling better you are my favorite baseball player. Do you live on Pete Rose Street.

from,

David

Pete Rose has a street named for him, it is near Western Hills High School in Cincinnati.

Dear Mr. Rose:

Enclosed please find a letter from one of your most avid fans. We were watching the series last night and David asked me if you knew that he really liked you.

Dear Pete   **31**

So not to disappoint him I told him that you probably knew that there were a lot of 6 year old boys who think he is the best ball player ever. Unfortunately that answer didn't satisfy him, he wanted to be sure that you knew that he personally liked you. So, that is the reason for this letter.

It may seem rather incredible that a lad so young would take such an interest in baseball, but David has been playing ball since he was old enough to hold a ball. He can name any player on the Reds team along with their number and position they play.

David has a scrap album with quite a few pictures of you in it. Especially where you are making head first dives. I know you are busy, but would it be at all possible for you to send him a picture of yourself. He would be thrilled to death to even think you thought of him.

Hope you are over the flu! Thank you for taking time to read these letters.

Sincerely,

Mrs. ?

Thank you for telling Pete how much David thinks of him. Many youngsters, like yours, admire Pete and his great baseball hustle. Hope the autographed picture made David happy.

Dear Mr. Rose:

I am a sixty one year old great grandmother and never miss a "Reds" game when it is on T. V. I have five grandsons and they all played baseball. My youngest one has been picked on the all stars every year he has played. You are his "Idle" he says someday I am going to play like Pete Rose, all his team mates

and fans will hollar come on "Pete". He plays first base until
they need him somewhere else.

    I would sure like to bring him and watch you play in the
World Series if I could afford it but as I can't will have to settle
watching on T.V, but I'll sure be doing that and rooting for the
"Reds".

    I am sure you are too busy to read this but I just wanted to
write you. You have a wonderful family I know you are proud
of. I admire you so for taking intrest in your son. My grandsons
haven't had a father to help them.

    A fan rooting for the "Reds"
    Mrs. L. T.

I sincerely hope that this great lady's grandson received his picture.

Dear Pete Rose "Charlie Hustle,"

    I really like the way you hustle. And most of all the way you
slide head first. Doesn't it hurt sometimes? You have an
exellent batting average. I have a 17" by 34" color poster of
you. Pretty soon I know you'll be in the Hall of Fame. I also
know your going to get three thousand hits, I am really rooting
for you. I would be super happy if I could have an autographed
picture of you. And I would really treasure it.

    I watched every game of the World Series. I really liked the
way you played Mickey Rivers to bunt. Man, you sure made
Rivers hit away.

    Howard

Pete got his 3,000th hit in May of '78. He was so proud that his good friend Tony Perez was standing on first base when he got it. The Reds were playing the Expos!

Dear Mr. Rose:

Before I ask a favor of you, please allow me to say Congratualtions for bringing the fans of Cincinnati another World Series Championship. You and the other players are surely a credit to all of baseball. I know in my heart 1977 will be a repeat of 1975 and 1976.!

I am a 40 year old man, but a 40 year old kid when it comes to the Reds. I started parking cars in the late 40's and peeking thru the holes in the wall at Crosley Field. I am now in prison and would love to have a picture of The Big Red Machine. If not a team picture, then one of you. I have no family or friends to get one for me, nor visitors that I could ask this favor of. And by the time I am to be released, I'm afraid this team in particular will be gone.

In closing, may I thank you for many hours you have brought to me in this lonely prison. I realize that baseball is your living, I am just so thankful you choose it!! So long, good luck, God bless you and yours, and I'll be listening in at Tampa!

Respectfully,
LeRoy

A picture was sent to this gentleman and I hope he enjoyed it.

Pete please read this.

I am writing to you Pete because I think you are the toughest in baseball ever. And always will be to me. Other people say

*that you are not the best. I still say you are. My family kid me
because I always have liked you. They say that you are not the
best. They are wrong "right". Other people say you will not send
autographed pitcures of you. I believe you will because the best
always sends their pictures to fans.*

*I went to Cincinnati to see you when you played the Pirates.
You smashed a double in the first inning.*

*I wanted to go and get your autograph but I couldn't get
passed the ushers. If you don't send me the autograph, will you
please autograph this paper and write me a letter about
yourself. I have had dreams of growing up just like you.
Because I want to be tough just like you. Please write.*

You best fan,
Everett

It's almost impossible to get down to field level from
second and third levels at Riverfront Stadium in Cincinnati. I think this holds true at most stadiums. The
ushers are doing their jobs when they say "no." Many
fans go to the bottom gates of the stadium and wait for
the players to come out to get their autographs. Sometimes the players are tired from playing in extreme heat
and have been at the stadium many hours, so all fans
should try and understand when they are refused.
These great guys really try to please their fans.

Dear Pete Rose,
*I am a big fan of yours. I like the Cinncinati Reds very much.
I had a bet with some Kids in school that the Reds would win
and of course, you know I won the bets.*

You probably know why I am writing but if you don't it is

that I would like a picture autograph of you.
I hope you send it soon.
Your Fan,
Michael

Dear Pete,
I am a good friend of David ——— and I've been a fan of yours for three years. You and the Reds have been my favorite for a long time. I've been with you all the way through the world series and wish you good luck! I have a lot of pictures of you from magazines and Sports Illustrated. I have a collection of baseball cards of you since the year 1972. I especially have a lot of action plays of you. I would be very happy if you could return this letter with your home address on it & autographed by some others like Johnny bench if you could.
From,
Jonathan

Dear Pete,
I think your the best player of all time. Hope you are going to the Hall of Fame. I love to watch you hit homers, bunt, make spectacular catches in the outfield and make super plays at third base. That catch in the All Star Game last year I was jumping out of my chair at home. I thought you were going to win the most valuble players award. Well anyways, I'm glad the Reds won the World Series. I hope you win it again. You are my favorite players because you never give up until 3 outs after 9½ innnings. When you hit a homerun at San Diego against the Padres I was cheering you all the way. I hope you hit so many homeruns against the Dodgers and beat them every game in the 1976 season.

Please send me your picture with your personally autograph please. Good-bye Pete.

  Yours truly,
   Dale

Baseball cards and action pictures are very popular collection items for the youngsters. Sorry, Pete's phone number and home address are no-no's. We get boxes full of mail every month. When someone secures Pete's home address, it is passed along and the mail comes rolling in to his house. One little fellow wrote that he bought it. Doesn't suprise me! The stadium address is the right address to use. Pete gets the mail there. In fact, that's the right place to write for all autographs, but one letter for each autograph to the individual players wanted, please.

I do not think that there's a doubt in anyone's mind about Pete being elected to "The Hall of Fame." He is a super ballplayer.

Mr. Rose,

  I recently saw you on the Mike Douglas show and would like to know where and for how much I can get a couple of those Pete Rose tee shirts for my 2½ yr. old son who idolizes and mimics you. I'd appreciate an autographed picture for my son.

  Mr. Alan —

Many people write about the tee-shirts. Some stadium concessionaires carry them, or you can get one made special at some sports shops or tee-shirt stores.

Dear Pete,

I'm so happy for you and the rest of the Reds. The world finally realizes how awsome the Cincinnati Reds are! Many of the Reds All-Stars are MVP candidates, and I'm proud of you all.

I totally agree with Bob Housam and Sparky Anderson on the DH and the new Basic Agreement. It scares me. Its ruining baseball. I sure hope it doesn't ruin the great Reds team that Mr. Housam worked so hard and so long to put together.

I live and die with all of you. That is why I'm asking you to please get me some autographs of your teammates. I know you can't get all 26 plus the 4 coaches and Sparky, but I would appreciate anything you can get — even if it is just yours that you can get. I greatly admire your wife, Karolyn, too and would like her autograph.

A Reds fan forever,
Linda

I will agree, Bob Howsam put together a terrific team, trading and adding until he had the perfect blend of players. What years 1975 and 1976 proved to be! Then the trades started and the team's enthusiasm dissipated. That's all changing again, now that Pete is the manager.

Pete Rose and team,

You guys are my faverote team. You guys let the yankees have it. Do you think could send some cards of something of you guys. I don't think too good cause I'm only 9 years old. I already have cards of Perez, Bench, and Gullet. I also have Mcenaney. I lost Norman and Plummer. And Pete, My mom says you're funny when you make faces at the umpire. And I a card of Joe Morgan for stealing 2nd most bases. Pete, your baseball card is hard to get.

> *See ya on T.V*
> *Your best fan,*
> *Jed*

You are so right, Pete's cards are hard to get. I bought umpteen packs of gum, trying to get Pete's card. My kids and I chewed the gum at the ballgames. You should see me blow bubbles!

Dear Pete Rose,

Hi! I'm a 13 year old girl who lives in Illinois and doesn't get to see many Reds games, but if any are on T.V. here you can bet I am watching them!

I think you are a very good player, and a very nice person. I don't think you know how many kids my age like you and the whole Reds team. Whenever I am in Ohio I make sure to watch all the Reds games on T.V. Next season I would really like to go see one at the stadium. I collect everything I can about the Reds for my scrap Book.

Would you please send me an autographed picture of you? I would really like that. I know you will read this letter and if I am lucky you might write back. My favorites on the team are you Johnny Bench and Joe Morgan, and Sparky Anderson! Well 'gotta' go. Please write back.

> *Sincerely,*
> *Julie!*

P.S. My Mom likes you too! She's from Ohio.

I can vouch for the fact that many thousands of children look up to Pete. They think he is the greatest and try to pattern their young lives after his hustle. He is their inspiration and Pete loves them all.

Dear Pete Rose,

Me and my grandfather and my mother are probably you #1 fans. I really like you a lot and I'd like you to send me a poster of you and a signed post card. My mom likes you and had a poster of you and our last name is Ross and at work on Rose of your name they scribbled out the E and put an S to make it Pete Ross. Every time you get a hit my grandpa claps and yells my grandpa is 77 years old and when you get a homerun it's funny to see him jump around. I am on a baseball team and I play 3rd base and I watch you all the time to see if I can pick anything up. the very first year I played we won 1st but they didn't give trophys. last year we won a 2nd place trophy this year 1st. My 1st year I was on the team called the purple panthers ever since then I've played 3rd base so I've played 3 years. If they ever traded you to the Phillies everybody I know would write complaints.

Love,
Robin

Grandparents really get excited over ballgames. I'm a grandma, and I do; and so does my better half. If there is a super play, I'll yell and whistle and then I remind myself to sit down and be calm. Another super play and I'm yelling and whistling all over again. I think it's called baseball fever.

Dear Pete Rose,

You think I'm going to say your my favorite baseball but your not. Your my third favorite ballplayer. I'm not from Phillie or New York. I rooted for Cincinnati in the playoffs and World Serice. Tony Perez is good. Sparky Anderson might keep him. Driessen can't be designated hitter. Driesan used to play third. Where you are playing at. Then you switch over. Then Foster moves. He's not moving Geronimo over he goes in right. Where dose Griffey go? Is it true you might go to the phills? Is it true you want more money? I'm getting a book about you. Now you think I'm going to ask you may I have your autograph.

Michael

This type of letter makes me chuckle. One thing for sure, he's honest! And for another, he knows his baseball. Like all good fans, he's a second-guesser. I wonder what he feels about how Pete is managing the Reds.

Dear Mr. Rose,

I have always been a fan of yours since the first time I ever saw you play and since then you have always been an idol to me for I feel you are the greatest player ever. I truly feel that you are underrated player ever. One day I hope to be as good a player as you are. I've been practicing and now I can go from first to third on any hit, sometimes home.

Mr. Rose, one of the reasons I'm writing this letter is because I'm an autograph collector and I would truely be honored, if, when you have some spare time could you please autograph the enclosed card for my own private collection. These are not intended to be sold. However, I do trade my extras for other I don't have. Please.

Dear Pete 41

Thank you, your fan,
  SLB

Only one autograph was sent. Some fans wanted two, others ten. So Pete set a limit of one to a letter.

Mr. Pete Rose,
  My name is Rose ——— and this is the second time I have written you. the first time I had commented on your baseball jersey because it had my name and age on the back "Rose" and "14." I know someone must have gotten my letter because I've gotten the Red's Alert, and mail with orders for baseball bats!
  You seem to have ignored the question I asked in the first letter. I wanted to know if by any chance I could have one of your baseball jerseys with "Rose" and "14" on the back? If you cannot give one to me, please don't ignore it, send me a letter saying no, or even send me the package with the jersey in it!
  Thanks so much,
    Rose

A very demanding young lady! An autograph picture was sent. If Pete sent a jersey, a signed ball, glove, bat, poster, or hat to everyone who asked, I'm sure the postal employees would ask me to take an extended holiday. As it is, I keep them quite busy sending out the letters with autographs.

Dear Pete,
  You're the best all-around ball player I have ever seen! It's unbelievable how you can keep hustling day after day like that.

Next to Butch Wynegar of the Twins you're my favorite ballplayer. I have a scrapbook of baseball things and whenever I see a picture of you, Butch Wynegar, or Johnny Bench I always cut it out of the paper, Sports Illustrated, or Sporting News. I've read your book "Charlie Hustle" and I really enjoyed it.

I hope it wouldn't be to much trouble if you could send me an autographed picture of yourself. If its to much trouble, skip it.

Thanks
Paul

Here's a lad who wants to trouble no one, but would really enjoy an autograph. I hope he enjoyed the picture.

Speaking of hustling every day, when Tony and I visited Los Angeles to see the Reds play, Pete treated us to lunch. It was mid-September and he stated that toward the end of the season, everyone was tired. The players were not hustling, but they should really try to give it their best shot. It's their job.

Pete looked at us and said, "Even the fans get tired. Look at you two. You've covered every game, and I know you are tired. Yet, you come to give us support."

He was so right; we were tired. But oh, how we loved it, seeing our favorite team, and especially Pete, play. Baseball is exciting!

3

No One's Perfect

Pete was having an idyllic youth until one day he learned that life has no free lunches, that there are dues to pay and work to be done if you want to succeed.

Some people call Pete a *showboater*, but he has never claimed to be the only hustler in baseball. His personal history speaks for itself, especially his teen years at Western Hills High School. That period in his life was nothing to brag about, and Pete has said as much.

"Most guys go through high school in four years. It took me five. I was so involved in sports in high school that I let the studies slide. I'm not proud of that. I point it out just to show you that I'm not as great as people say I am. In high school I forgot to hustle academically. I slowed down. Well, I've learned my lesson. I've been running ever since."

Pete started high school in the fall of 1955, and as he put it, "They sprung me in 1960." He recounts the years by how the Reds finished each season and under which manager. By the time graduation day came along, the late Fred Hutchinson was guiding the Reds to a sixth place finish, and by the end of that year, Pete was under contract to the team.

That first year at Western Hills High School was almost heaven for Pete. He went out for everything but the girls' swimming team. He played halfback on the freshman football team, guard on the basketball team, and was catcher on the baseball team. He didn't play the first two football games because his coach was concerned that he might get hurt, Pete being such a lightweight. But he did get to play and accounted for himself well.

In his spare time, he was boxing or at least trying to. He had two fights and lost both of them. One bout was against a man more than twice his age. Candy Jamison was 30 years old and seven of his own children sat at ringside to watch the match.

His sophomore year wasn't exactly what Pete had hoped it would be. He wasn't asked to play varsity football that summer, and this upset Pete. He then did what most teenagers do when denied something they consider more important that life itself: he rebelled. The end result of his personal guerrilla war against authority is best described by Pete:

"I did a lot of dumb things that I regret even today. I'd start our for school and I'd never get there. That shows how dumb I was. Or I'd go to school a half a day and then, with a couple of other guys, cut out. We'd bum around, go downtown, see a movie, or just bum. The guys felt they'd got the same bum deal. Yeah, we really went around in those days feeling sorry for each other. I think that's the only thing I really regret in my whole life, that I wasn't a good scholar, the way my dad was. But I think I could have been if I wanted to be. Only I was too interested in feeling sorry for myself."

It seemed to Pete that he spent almost as much time in the assistant principal's office as he did in the classroom. It wasn't that he did anything so awful. It was a lot of little things; mostly being late for classes, skipping classes, shooting rubberbands in class, or fighting. The guy who hustles also is a scrapper. Billy Martin is a good example of that. He was a hustler during his playing days, just as Pete is. But back then, Pete was a kid from a neighborhood that was rougher than most. He didn't belong to a street gang or anything of that nature. He simply took his frustration out on anyone who got in his way.

As the year wore on and Pete would see other guys playing sports, he became even more rebellious, to the point where he really felt left out. "I was going the wrong way fast — and that's for sure." Things went from bad to worse until the year culminated with Pete flunking every subject except, of course, physical education. All the lectures from his father had fallen on deaf ears, and all Pete's promises to straighten up went unfulfilled.

That summer he played baseball. The long arm of the assistant principal office couldn't reach him then. But fall came again and reality set in. Back to school to have another go at the books. Maturity found its way into Pete and he applied all the lessons his father and uncle had taught him on the athletic field to the classroom. "The result: I grew up a lot, I got on some of the teams, and I was on the right track again."

Pete doesn't take all the credit for turning himself around in high school. There were other forces at work. Pete had what one might call a *personal monitor*. He called her "a *girl* body-guard" and his "den mother".

Her name was Jean Blankenship, and Pete wrote that "they appointed her to look after me and keep me out of trouble. I'd carry her books down the hall, meet her at her locker, and stuff like that. We'd go to lunch together. We'd be most everywhere together. I guess they figured if I was carrying her books I wouldn't be able to go around decking people. It worked, too. She was a real beauty. She was beautiful inside and out. She was one of the top girls in school. But she was older than me — and to her I was just a dumb kid brother. She was really okay."

To this day, Pete is well aware of how close he came "to flushing everything down the drain."

Pete fared well on the varsity football team for two years. In one of those years, Western Hills won a championship, and Pete is proud that he had something to do with it. Always a team player, it made no difference to him who scored the touchdowns. What mattered was winning, and he still has that attitude.

Like schools all across America, Western Hills had a place — a drive-in restaurant, canteen, whatever — where the kids went after the games. For Pete and his friends it was Frisch's where they sold double-decked hamburgers. After each game the restaurant always held more people that it could hold; everyone filling up on Cokes and burgers, a few kids crying in their malteds because Western Hills had blown another game. It was a very noisy and wonderful high school hangout. The place smelled of French fries, hamburgers, girls' perfume, and milk shakes. "That was living," as Pete put it.

By the time Pete reached his senior year at Western Hills High School he was pretty much back in everyone's good graces. His grades weren't the best in school, but he was passing. His parents stopped worrying about him turning into a bum.

The only sad part about that year was Pete was ineligible to play on any of the high school teams. Four years of eligibility is all anyone gets. He did assist the coaches whenever he could, but that wasn't the same as playing. "I don't dig sideline action. Only there I was, sidelined. It wasn't anyone's fault but my own." But Pete did have a good thing going that senior year.

Pete was one of a few young men who were allowed to put on a Reds' uniform and catch fly balls while the Reds held batting practice at the stadium. He considers that to be his fondest memory of that last year of school.

There was one other thing he recalls with good feeling. His first car. A 1937 Plymouth with no front bumper. It had a radio, a stick shift, and was dark blue. And it only had 35,000 miles on it. "But it looked so funny without that front bumper that when I brought it home my mother looked out the window and laughed. Mothers don't know too much about cars, do they? Even though it had running boards she kept laughing because she just couldn't believe that I paid a hundred bucks for it. Anyway, there I was shagging fly balls at the Reds' batting practice. And there I was, wearing a Reds' uniform. That was the greatest, really."

Pete's dad descirbed his own feelings in an interview about the time Pete started working out with the Reds.

"John Brosnan was responsible for Pete getting down to the ball park," my dad told an interviewer. "John knew more about kids who played ball at Western Hills High School than anybody else knew. John seemed to have his own personal encyclopedia on any kids who played ball at Western Hills or Elder or even in the Knot Hole Leagues. Listen, John knew each kid's family and each kid's history. He was always around for practice. If a kid hit a ball and it went out in the street at Western Hills, John would trot out and bring it back. See, he sort of worked for the Reds in a bird-dog kind of job. He was the one who fixed it so Pete could go down there afternoons and work out in a Reds' uniform. This was big stuff to me. The first afternoon Pete was down there, I rushed out to the ball park as soon as I got off from work. I didn't know then about getting in at the pass gate. I went to the front and asked the ticket seller how soon I could get into the park. He said they didn't open till six. And Pete had been there since four. So I paced up and down until six, went in, and there was Pete — in uniform. I choked up. You know, there was my boy in uniform.

"I felt that if Pete never takes another step in base-ball, at least I saw him in a major league uniform."

You would think a boy — a young man — who was having his dream come true would never do anything that might make that dream come to a sudden halt. Well, Pete almost did.

One afternoon he chose to go see a girl instead of going out to Crosley Field to shag flies. His father showed up and found Pete not there. Harry Rose called home and learned that Pete had gone to see a girl. Harry told his wife to call Pete at the girl's house and tell him "to get the hell to the ball park."

And that was the day he first met Fred Hutchinson. He saw him from a distance in the locker room when he walked through. Their first meeting was very casual. No matter. Hutchinson was to be, for Pete, just about the most important guy in the world. He was the man who made the "Big Time" happen for Pete. And he was the guy who, when he died, broke the heart of everybody who loved baseball. Hutchinson nodded to Pete as he passed through the locker room.

"I'll never forget that moment," said Pete. "And to think, I almost missed it completely because this chick had blue eyes and a funny way of cocking her head when she grinned."

4

The Man Who Cares

The general public does not know this, but Pete is a very kind and feeling person. He has visited many ill children across the country and brings a ray of sunshine and hope into their young lives. Pete rarely talks about it; for it is one of his private commitments. The press seldom mentions this very human side of Pete. It's more fun to write about the rough and ready side that you see on the baseball field.

Dear Pete,

We want to express our gratitude to you for the personal visit you made to our son during your last appearance in Huntington on January 30th.

Tom passed away on February 1st within 36 hours of your visit with him at St. Mary's Hospital. He was a very brave young man who suffered constantly but never complained during his 17 years of life. Your willingness to spend a few minutes with Tom during his last hours will be an everlasting memory to us and all of his family and friends.

Thank you and may God bless you and your family forever.

Gratefully,
  Mr. & Mrs. James

Hi,

Congratulations. I don't usually write letters like this but I thought you'd get a kick out of it. My boss passed himself off as a reporter for Channel 12 and was right in the locker room with your team and even attended your party. He got back to Albany at 5:30 in the morning and was so zooped up he came in to work to tell us all about it. He had a ball signed by you and your teammates (should have been two words, sorry). Well when I saw your name I gave it a big smack. One of the guys took it out of my hand and spat on it. Well that did it, being the lady that I am I slugged him. Lucky for me he didn't hit back cause he'd have killed me.

As you can tell by the above I am a fan of yours — so are my two brothers. I was the only one in the office besides my crazy boss who was for Cincinnati (not crazy cause he was for your team, but crazy cause of the antics he pulls). Oh I forgot to tell you what else he did, when you and Thurman were being interviewed before game 4 he was standing right in back of you. He said a guy had did that the night before and was thrown out of the park. He said Yogi attended the party (only good sport on the other team). He also saw Joe DiMaggio but was afraid to approach him. That I find hard to believe, but he said he has a way about him that you just don't go up and slap him on the back. He told me you gave your shirt away and that you were really nice. That made up for all the flack I took from the rest of the office who naturally were Yankee fans and said they

HATED you. I told them they were just jealous.

By the way been watching you Geritol commercial and tell your wife I think she is beautiful.

Best wishes to you, your wife, and children.

See you next year.

Betty

P.S. I work for the state — can't you tell?

Dear Mr. Rose

I wish to thank you and the rest of the Reds for the many hours of pleasure you have given me watching your baseball games on T.V.

I have never seen a "live" big league ball game but next year the Blue Jays will be playing in this locality, I expect to see them play other teams in the American League which sorry to observe will not include the Reds so I shall continue to admire them on T.V.

I have enclosed an interesting cartoon of the entertainment section of the Toronto Globe & Mail perhaps you have already received a great many of these cartoons. The artist has done a good job of uglifying you as the symbol of the Reds, but his respect for the team as well as you shows through. I hope you like it.

Congratulations and many thanks.

Sincerely,

Art

Dear Pete Rose,

I'm sorry Don Gullet broke his ankle in the world series. I'm also sorry you hit so good. You played the field O.K.

I like the way you bat. I'm trying to switch hit. So far I can hit it the ball out in the outfield. I'm right handed.

The places I played is third base, pitcher, shortstop, second base, first base, centerfield. I liked pitching the best because that's what I've been wanting to be. I liked third and I played third the most.

Our team won the championship and after that. I got picked to go to North Vernon to play. And Seymour came in third. I got a big hit durring the game. And I got hit 4 times in three games.

This summer I came to watch you play and you got a home run on errors. You guys won 11 to 10. Before you guys won. The other teams coach brought in one of the outfielders and there was 2 outfields and 7 infielders. My age is 10. And I'm sure glad you guys won the series.

Your friend,
George

Dear Pete,

I am a very big fan of yours and have a big crush on you. I am very jealous of your wife Carolyn. I love the way that you play ball and you are really the best on the team. I love Don Gullett and Bill Plummer too. Tell Don, I'm very sorry about his ankle.

I have 24 tapes of you singing Aqua Velva. I think you are so cute! There's a guy at school named Scott, that is short and looks exactly like you. I have a crush on him, too, but I love you, alot. (I love the way you dive to get on a base). Other people I like are 1. Pete Rose! 2. Mark Fidrych 3. Steve Yeager 4. Don Gullett 5. Larry Bowa 6. Tom Underwood 7. Bill Plummer and George Brett and many more!

But you're number 1 with me! Please, don't quit baseball

because they say you're too old. 35 is a great age! And April 14 is great. It's you birthdate, your uniform number, my age, my birthday number and my favorite number. Stay with the Reds and please write back!!

Lots of love!
Yours forever
Jean

To Charlie Hustle or better known as Pete Rose,

Pete don't think this is a letter bomb just because I'm from New York. I felt the same way you did, when they hit you with the bottle in the 1973 playoffs. You just not the greatest active player I seen but you are also my idol. I bought your Pete Rose winning baseball book and I have studied it. I think I am willing to do the things Charlie Hustle has done. I tried to do your head first slide and I almost killed myself. Rose don't worry one day I would get that magic touch and the head firt slide would be a success. I just admire seeing you play. Rose remember the day your was at Shea and your lost 1-0, a shutout by Koosman. Remember then your was getting on the bus and when the bus was ready to leave nobody wanted to open the gate unless you come out. Well I was part of that crowd. It wasn't that much of success becaus the cops came out and cleared the way. Rose if it's no trouble I would appreciate if you send me an autograph picture of the future Hall of Famer. Good luck in your future years.

Yours Truly
Harvey
P.S. Sorry for the mistakes.

Dear Pete   55

Dear Pete,
    I'm one of your fans. I'm glad the Reds won the series. I also like the way you clap for your yourself when no one claps for you. And I like the way you dive for the bases. I hope you play for many more years. And I especially like you when you hit a home run. Would you send me a picture of you please?
    Thank you,
     From Craig

Dear Pete Rose,
    Hi! My name is Carole and I'm writing to you because the Cincinnate Reds is my favorite baseball team and you are my favorite player. I think you are a great baseball player because you play ball with so much enthusiasm. Unfortunately I haven't been to Cincinnati yet to see a few games and to eat in your famous resteraunt but I hope to sometime next season. I understand how busy you must be but would you please send me an autographed picture. I would be very humored if you did so.
    Your fan,
     Carole

Pete had two restaurants in Cincinnati, one in the Western Hills area and one near Tri-County Shopping Center. I've been to both many times. He placed some of his trophies, including the Hickok Belt, in a display case at the newer restaurant. It is interesting to see.

Dear Pete Rose,
    Pete, how many homeruns have you hit? Where do you live? Could I have your autograph? My name is John.

You are my favorite player in the American and National League. What is your telephone number? Do you have any pets? Did you ever git picked for the most valuable player award? how dose it feel to have won the world Series? Do you have any kids?

From John

This letter asked Pete many questions. I sent an autographed picture to John. I'll try to fill in some of the answers to the questions for the fans that don't know these things about Pete.

A Doberman pinscher named "Dobby" is the family pet; he's a beautiful dog. The telephone number cannot be given out. it is changed quite frequently because, somehow, someone secures the number and passes it along. Then the calls come in and the number has to be changed to give the family some privacy. He won the Rookie-of-the-Year award in 1963, Most Valuable Player in 1973, and World Series M.V.P. in 1975. It is terrific to be a World Series winner. Pete has three adorable children: a daughter, Fawn, 20; and two sons, Petey 15, who is getting to be quite a ballplayer already, and Tyler Edward, 1, whom Pete calls "Smoogie".

5

Down in the Bushes

"There is contracts," said an outfielder Pete once knew, "and, on the other hand, there is contracts."

Pete concurs on that proposition wholeheartedly. Although he has signed several contracts over the years — the sum total of which is still confidential information, to be shared only by Pete and the IRS — there was no contract of his more gratifying to him than his first one with the Reds. It was in 1960, and Pete had just graduated from Western Hills High School.

During his senior year, since he wasn't eligible to play for the varsity at school, Pete played in the Dayton Amateur League for a team from Lebanon, Ohio. He was hitting .500 at the time he graduated from school. The league had games on Monday and Wednesday nights and Sunday afternoons. Pete was still in school when the league began play that year. In the daytime, he was in class trying to finish his education properly, and at night he was pounding out hits and making double-plays at second base.

In his first game, he felt he had to prove himself to everyone, including the water boy. He managed to get in on the business end of a couple of twin killings, and he got a hit. To say he felt cocky...? That's when his uncle Buddy took him down a few pegs.

"Don't get all excited," he cautioned. "Listen, Pete, just relax and play."

That was hard advice to take, but Pete took it. And on the strength of that, he started tearing up thát league.

Unbeknown to Pete his uncle had other things going for him. Neither did Pete know that at a lot of games there was a man named Jack Baker in the stands, keeping a close eye on him. He was a friend of Pete's uncle. Baker was a scout for the Baltimore Orioles. Both Baker and Uncle Buddy, who was scouting for the Reds, watched him go five-for-five one day. Baker wanted Pete for the Orioles, but he didn't know that Uncle Buddy had other plans for Pete.

Harry Rose knew what was happening behind the scenes, but he said nothing to Pete about it. He and Pete's uncle figured that knowing about the Orioles might upset Pete's game.

So the Friday night Pete was graduating from high school, Uncle Buddy showed up at Pete's house to tell him the news about the Reds wanting to talk to him about a contract. Pete was out celebrating his graduation. "That wonderful uncle of mine had given me the best graduation present anybody had ever given anybody anytime anywhere," said Pete.

The next day Pete and Harry met with Uncle Buddy, Phil Seghi, and a few of the other business-types from the Reds in the stands at Crosley Field. Seghi offered Pete $7,000 to sign, and he gave him the option of going into the minors at Geneva right away or waiting until the following spring to take his first shot at the Reds' minor league camp in Tampa. Pete, after some dickering by his father and uncle, made the final decision.

"I'd like to sign," said Pete. "I'd like to sign and go right now."

And that was that!

The time between his signing and the airplane's departure for Geneva, New York on Monday seemed to last forever. Pete and his dad went to the little golf course at Saylor Park and played a little, but Pete's mind wasn't on the game. The Roses' telephone never stopped ringing. The news had been on the radio and there it was: hometown boy signs with Cincinnati Reds. And come Monday he was on the plane, his first air-trip ever to anywhere.

Major League Baseball wasn't always the best way to make a living, and the Minor Leagues were worse. When Pete started out, he was making $400 a month. Out of that he had to pay his living expenses — room and board, clothing, whatever. On the road, the team payed the hotel bills but room only. At Geneva, Pete got $3 a day to eat on.

There was no welcoming committee to greet Pete when he stepped off the bus in Geneva, a town of less than 18,000 people in the Lehigh Valley on the northern end of Lake Seneca, 40 miles from Rochester, 50 from Syracuse, and 30 from Lake Ontario. The distance from the urban life he had known growing up and his home being more than 500 miles to the southwest made Pete a very lonely ballplayer that first year as a pro.

Pete went straight from the bus station to the ball park. The other players were there, but they all had cold shoulders. After that reception, Pete was taken to a hotel for the night.

The next day things were different. Pete met Tony Perez for the first time and ran into Ron Flender, another Cincinnatian that he had known. Pete had hoped to room with Flender, but no such luck; Flender was married. But by the end of the day, Pete had made new living arrangements, sharing a place with three other players: Jack Irwin, John Truex, and Larry Souel.

Pete didn't start burning up the league like he had been doing, playing semi-pro back in Ohio. His fielding was so-so, but his hitting was worse. But the coaches worked with him, giving him lots of extra batting practice whenever the opportunity was there. Day after day, they pounded hitting wisdom into him, and Pete learned.

But Pete didn't progress as fast as he thought. The coaches had other ideas. The reports they were sending back to Cincinnati were not good.

He was only an adequate second baseman, replacing Tony Perez at that position on orders from the Reds home office. His hitting was only average. By the end of the season in Geneva, a lot of people were convinced that Pete was due for a short pro career.

Pete related a conversation with his father after the baseball season ended that fairly well sums up his attitude at the time:

"I remember sitting around home, fresh from Geneva, and they had this football game going over there by the ferry. I ached to get out there and play.

" 'You might get hurt,' my dad said, 'and put an end to everything.'

" 'I said nothing.

" 'If you get hurt,' my dad said, 'the ball club is sure to find out about it. They might think they got themselves a pretty dumb athlete who goes out and hurts himself in a game of scrub football.'

" 'Dad,' I said.

" 'Yes?'

" 'What did *you* use to tell everybody?'

" 'When?' he said.

" 'When they said you were crazy, you the father of four kids, out there playing football with guys half your age. And they went around saying you'd be hurt. What did you used to tell them?'

"He gave me a funny look. 'I'd tell them that there isn't a man in the world who could hurt me on the football field. I'd tell them . . . '

"He stopped and smiled.

" 'If I was like that,' he said, 'how can I expect you to be any different?'

" 'So?'

" 'Go on out there,' he said, 'and show them how it's played. Only, Pete, one thing.'

' "What's that?'

" 'Don't forget to hustle.' "

Harry Rose received a rude awakening during Pete's first year of pro ball. It happened in Cincinnati when he ran into someone from the Reds' front office who had some scouting reports with him. Harry asked him how Pete was doing. The guy said nothing, merely handing Harry one of the reports which read: "Pete Rose can't make a double play, can't throw, can't hit left-handed, and can't run."

When Pete was assigned to the Jersey City roster that winter, Harry was breathing easier.

Pete reported to the club in Tampa the next spring. The Jersey City team had been in Havana the year before. The franchise was moved when Fidel Castro took power in Cuba. The team was made up of mostly Blacks, and the manager was named Nat Reyes.

Although Pete was on the Jersey City roster at the beginning of spring training, he didn't play there that year. Instead he was sent down to the Tampa Tarpons in the Class D Florida State League. Johnny (Double No-Hit) Vander Meer was the manager.

"I remember that first day well," said Vander Meer. "The big team was gone north and I was given this bunch of raw rookies. We divided up for a game so we could get a first look at them.

"Up came this kid Rose. He got a base on balls. He ran down to first. Hmmm, I thought. Next time up he got a base hit and he ran to first. Next time up he hit a routine infield grounder. He ran to first. Hmmm. Next time up he hit a fly ball to the outfield and ran to first.

"Afterwards in the clubhouse I went up to him and asked, 'You run to first everytime you get a walk?'

" 'Yes, sir, I'm just looking for a job.'

"I said to Rose, 'You keep on running son and you're liable to get one.'"

Pete got off to a good start, and by the time he had played 15 games he had a dozen triples. And the publicity started coming hot and heavy. By the end of the first month, Pete was batting a solid .350.

Pete wrote that the publicity was inspiring, but the presence of his mother at the games was even more so. The day he broke his own personal record for triples, his mother was there, and he presented her with the ball. He wound up hitting 30 triples that year, a record that still stands.

His work at Tampa resulted in an opportunity to play in the instructional league that winter, which then helped to move him up from Class D to Class A. Being named Minor League Player of the Year for the Florida State League didn't hurt his chances either.

But Pete was a second baseman, and the Reds' farm system was loaded with quality second sackers. Tommy Harper was the Minor League Player of the Year that same year in the Three I League at Topeka where he played under Dave Bristol, and so was Cesar Tovar, who had been named Minor League Player of the Year in the Pin League.

The next year Pete played second base at Macon, Georgia under Dave Bristol. He had another great year, hitting 17 triples and leading the league in triples as well as setting an all-time record for runs scored with 136 in 138 games. He also had 35 doubles and batted .330.

There was talk during the season of Pete moving up to San Diego, the Reds' Triple A team in the Pacific

Coast League. But that's all it was — talk. Pete played the whole year in Macon. Tommy Harper was the second baseman for San Diego.

Altogether Pete played two and a half years in the minor leagues. A half year at Geneva at Class D, a full year at Tampa, also Class D, and a year at Macon, Class A. Along with those seasons, he spent two winters in the instructional league in Florida. His second stint in the learning league was after his season at Macon. The following spring he finally put on a Cincinnati Reds uniform.

Life in the bush leagues was hard, but it was also fun. The money wasn't much, and the living arrangements weren't the greatest. And travel? No chartered jets for the minors. The lower the league in the minor league structure, the lower the form of travel.

But not everybody made even the minors. Pete's father told the story of three young men from Cincinnati who had been signed by the Reds. They reported to Tampa when Pete was there on the Jersey City roster. One of them was a fellow named Bobby Steinbeck. In Pete's estimation, Bobby was a better ballplayer than he was, having been on rival high school teams back home. Bobby lasted three weeks before being released. The only explanation Pete had was Bobby was over-awed by the magnitude of being in Tampa among all those players who had already gained some experience in the pros. The competition, evidently, proved to be too much for him to take.

"Probably the loneliest sight in the world is to see a guy who has been released, killing time at the ball park, watching the rest of us work out, while he stands there in civvies, hanging onto his suitcase, and waiting for the bus that will take him away from everything he'd ever dreamed of. When you're out on the field, you try not to look. That could be you, standing there, on the outside, looking in. And you get a gut feeling because there are no guarantees in baseball. That's him today. Tomorrow it could — for real — be you. So you practice a little harder and pretend baseball will always be there. And you know inside it won't. So you hustle harder to make the dream last."

And, of course, there was the fun side life in the minors. Pete had more than his share of memorable experiences, and he's got lots of humorous stories. One of his favorites is the time former major league pitcher Mel Queen played a practical joke on a player from Venezuela while they were playing for the Macon team.

It seems that Macon, Georgia has more than its share of frogs, and it also rains abundantly there, thereby bringing out the frogs in droves. The Venezuelan hated frogs, and everyone knew it, especially Queen who was an outfielder in those days. Queen and the teammate were in the outfield together exchanging practice throws. Before the game, Queen had taped a frog to a baseball and had stashed it in rightfield. He got his "frog-ball" and threw it to the Venezuelan who caught it, saw the frog, dropped the ball, threw away his glove, and took off running. It took more than a little coaxing to get the Venezuelan back into the game.

Traveling by car more often than not in the minors, the young players learned a lot about the highways and byways of America, including where all the speed traps were located. Pete tells the story of how he learned about a speed trap the hard way.

"One time my mother and dad brought my new Corvette to Knoxville where we were playing and Dave Bristol said sure, I could run it back to Macon. I guess Bristol figured I'd be safer inside a car than on top of one, which I did once to scare the pants off the other guys. What happened was, there were eight of us jammed in a station wagon, the long night haul was a drag, and there I was, piled in back on top of the equipment, so to break the monotony I sneaked the back window open. Then, when the guys weren't noticing, I climbed out the back window — while the wagon was zipping along in the sixties — and I climbed up on the roof of the wagon to ride awhile there, which was cool and good. After I did this for a while, I got bored, so I leaned down over the front windshield and waved at the driver. The poor guy almost flipped. So you can see why Dave Bristol figured it would be better for me to drive *inside* my own car rather than ride atop one of theirs. So there Helms and I were, tooling back to Macon in my Corvette, and I got so pleased with the way it was running, I passed a car in a no-passing zone somewhere in the night. All of a sudden the car I passed turned into a police car. Its driver picked up a red light he had on the seat beside him, plugged it in, and that was all, brother. There was this kangaroo court and it cost us about eighty dollars. Luckily we were close to home because that took all the cash we had. All we had between us and home was a half tank of gas."

So life in the minor leagues was tough and kind and fun and work and play, but most of all it was memorable, an experience that no ballplayer, especially Pete, would trade.

And the minors are a stepping stone to the ultimate goal of every kid who loves baseball. Every kid wants to play in the Major Leagues, and Pete was no different.

But Pete wasn't in the Majors yet. He didn't even have a major league contract. when he put on a Reds uniform for the first time during that spring of 1963.

At the winter meetings before the season, Reds' Manager Fred Hutchinson remarked that he had been very impressed by Pete in the winter league. "If I had any guts," said Hutch, "I'd stick Rose on second and forget about him."

Pete went to camp with the same determination and dedication he has always displayed. And it paid off.

When an exhibition game against the Chicago White Sox started, Pete, who wasn't in the starting lineup, went to another diamond with some other reserves and took some batting practice. But instead of leaving when he was through hitting, he went back to the dugout, and Hutchinson put him in as a pinchrunner for Wally Post in the ninth inning of a scoreless game. Two innings later Pete doubled in his first at-bat in a Reds' uniform. In the fourteenth inning he doubled again and scored the game's only run.

That performance left an indelible impression in Hutchinson's mind.

Later that spring the Reds were playing the Yankees. Pete came up to bat, took four balls, and ran to first base. He'd been running to first on walks ever since he saw Enos Slaughter do it on television and his dad remarked, "That's the way baseball ought to be played." The idea made sense to Pete.

But Yankee star Mickey Mantle hadn't seen Pete do it before. He and Whitey Ford began some catcalling, and Mantle yelled out, "Hey, you, Charlie Hustle!" The writers picked it up, and it's stuck ever since.

That spring Pete was sent with the split squad to Mexico City to play a series of games. He didn't fair too well, going 2 for 20, but the first game back Hutchinson stuck him in the starting lineup when the Reds played the Dodgers in Vero Beach. Pete began to shine then, and he remained with the big team all the way through spring training.

But he still didn't have a contract to play for the Reds, not even when the team arrived in Charleston, West Virginia for their final exhibition game. Pete had heard rumors from sportswriters that he would be given a contract and taken with the team to Cincinnati for the traditional major league opening game. Pete could only hope, but that hope seemed to dwindle as the day wore on. Then that night he signed his first major league contract in Charleston. He related that it meant more to him that his father got such a great thrill out of it. "My dad, back at home, heard it on the radio. I guess that was the greatest newscast he'd ever heard."

Pete couldn't be sure of it then, but the minors were behind him for good. He had served his apprenticeship, and now it was time for him to step into the limelight in Cincinnati. The hometown boy had come home.

6

"This is for you, Pete!"

I would like to share with you some of the things that have come to Pete via the postman:

1) A box, securely wrapped and tied. We very carefully unwrapped it. The box was about 6 inches long and 6 inches wide, stuffed with paper. It contained *one* hat pin and a note that was very sincere. An elderly lady wanted to be sure Pete's hat would never blow off again as he ran the bases. She had no idea that the players wear hard safety hats to protect their heads.

2) A letter with a candy bar enclosed. It was sent to the stadium (it was summer), and stayed there until we picked up the mail and brought it home. Talk about a mess; melted chocolate everywhere!

3) Chewing gum that was overheated and messy.

4) Beautifully hand-drawn pictures of Pete. The sender obviously spent several hours drawing them. Pete was so pleased with them.

5) Several imprinted tee-shirts.

6) Pins with pictures of a rose on them.

7) Snapshots of boys and girls, some in baseball uniforms, wanting Pete to see what they looked like.

9) Term papers from school, some with the complete history of Pete, or his baseball statistics to date. They did their homework, and most had received an A. They wanted Pete to read, autograph, and return the papers to them.

10) Remember the underwear commercial? Some fans sent enlarged pictures (some framed) to be autographed. They enclosed special envelopes and postage for their return. I wonder where they have them hanging?

11) A fan from the West Coast sent a rabbit fur. He also apoligized since the rattles from a rattlesnake could not be sent this time — his dog ate them.

12) Small statuettes made from dough, but were broken by the time we received them.

13) Many hand made pictures from fans expressing their love for Pete.

14) A letter from a girl stating, "Pete, I love You! Will you marry me?" Pete really got a kick out of that one.

In 1977 I took what I thought were the interesting letters and made Pete a scrapbook as a surprise gift.

Dear Pete Rose,
I think that belt you got is the most valuable thing in the whole wide world. When I was in the hospital you sent a signed picture — thank you. Thanks for wining the World Series.
Your's truly
Doug

That "Belt" is a very valuable award. Pete is very honored to have received it. I do hope the picture made your hospital stay a little more pleasant.

Dear Pete,
How've you been? How's your family? Have you been very busy lately? I bought aqua vela for my father because you use it. And if you use it I want my father to use it. I got a rabbit and I named it Peteie. Well gotta go. Bye for now. I'll write soon.
Love Always,
Debbie

Has Pete been busy lately? He has so many things to do, personal appearances, making commercials for T.V., spending time with his family. From the time spring training starts until the last game of the season, eight months are dedicated to his job of playing baseball! Glad you like Aqua Velva, and yes, Pete uses it. I have the bottle taken from his locker at Riverfront. It is half full.

Pete Rose,
Have you ever heard the saying: "Nice guys finish last"? That explains why you're first. I refer to one instance upon which Willie Montanez was at bat, Davey May at second. Mr. Montanez hit the ball over first and was out when he reached the base. Mr. May went sliding into second. It is my understanding that you called out to him that it was a foul ball. Upon returning to first he was tagged out. I do not in the slightest bit find this amusing or funny. The way I see it you represent an example of bad sportsmanship.

Second, one day on a television show you were asked to sing your "Aqua Velva Song." You replied with the answer, "No, I'm not getting paid for it." Once again totally uncalled for.

Last but not least, upon returning to Cincinnati after the World Series I saw a picture of you with a Yankee hat on and thumbs turned down. Again, unnecessary! Fact it Pete Rose, that's three strikes and you're out.

An Atlanta Brave Fan Forever

I was at the game when Pete fooled May into an out. In fact, I just opened my scrapbook and read the newspaper clipping. The headline reads, "Sneaky Pete dupes Braves outfielder." It only proves some people are more clever than others, and when your livelihood depends on whether you win or lose, all is fair. Remember how other players tried to do the same thing to Pete in a previous chapter? It all works out; it's part of the game.

I love Pete, but he doesn't sound too good singing. I can't blame him for saying no, and why should he embarrass himself? About not getting paid for it? Even contestants on the "Gong Show" got something, so why shouldn't Pete?

The hat incident didn't hurt anyone. If Dale Murphy or Bob Horner of the Atlanta Braves had done the same thing, I wonder if this lady would have been as upset.

She didn't put her name to the letter, but she did enclose her return address.

Hi Pete:
I am sorry I have been so slow in telling how glad to learn of

Dear Pete 73

all the nice things happening to you. You really deserve them.

I was sorry to miss the Rosie Reds luncheon but on January 20 I was taken to Riverside Hopital with pneumonia and coronary heart-attack and just came home on February 7.

I will be with you all in spirit and listening to the radio broadcasts and I hope 1976 will be a better baseball year and the best of your life.

May God bless you and all the team and again win the National League Pennant and World Championships 1976.

Yours,

Mary

This lovely lady writes to Pete often giving him encouragement. Would it help to tell you she is 82 years young? Beautiful!

Dear Pete,

Thank you for the picture you sent my brother Chad.

Could you please send me one, too?

My name is Jamie ———, and since I am only 4½, my dad is helping me write this letter.

Thank you very much.

Jamie

P.S. We used to live in Ohio (Marietta) and have always been Reds fans!

Oops! If I know there are two children, I try to send two pictures. Having five children of my own, I know the problems. Jamie, enjoy your picture of Pete.

Dear Sir,

2 or 3 months ago I sent you a birthday card and you sent me back a personalized autograph on a Sincere Thank You card I'll cherish it for the rest of my life. But I bet you didn't know I was a teenager. Yup thats right. Not only am a a teenager I'm a girl (14 years old).

For the past two years we've been coming to Florida just to see the Cincinnati Reds springtrain. This year we're going and I hope to see you and Johnny Bench there.

Sincerely Yours,

Loraine

It was decided by Pete that a thank you should be sent for birthday cards sent to him. Girls like baseball too! I am so glad you liked the thank you card.

Dear Pete,

You have always been my favorite ballplayer and Person, because of all the things you have done for Cincinnati. You were born here and you still live here, and were glad you still do. I guess because you graduated from West Hi makes me even more fond of you, because I also graduated from there. I was really glad to see that they named West Hi driveway after you, you really deserve it.

When you where selected as SPORTSMAN of the YEAR by Sports Illustrated I wrote them and told them how much I agreed with thier choice. I have enclosed the letter that they sent me back.

I am a 20 year old guy who loves all sports especially baseball. I played knothole baseball, but I did not go on any longer playing on a team. I am sorry that I did not go on and

Dear Pete   **75**

*keep playing because I am pretty good. I tried to copy myself
and my attitude after you, because you're the BEST.*

*Thanks you everything Pete. I hope there are many more
years for NO. 14 in a Red's uniform.*

GOD BLESS and GOOD LUCK,

Sincerely yours,

Randy L.

Here is a young man complimenting Pete of his
hustle. The driveway named for Pete is at Western
Hills High School in Cincinnati. I never found it,
although I've looked for it. Most of Cincinnati thinks
Pete is great, a sure candidate for the "Hall of Fame."

Dear Pete,

*Do you know how the chances are at getting good seats
at Dodger Stadium on September 14 and 15th?*

*We are planning on going out West, and·can get seats in
Frisco and hopefully in San Diego — but don't know about
L.A.*

*Have most of the mail answered — only ½ mail bag left —
which is probably 800 to 1000 letters. I'm out of pictures. Send
some out with Gary — and if any more mail, will pick it up.*

Helen

Sometimes I have to write a note and pass it to Pete at
a game. He's a very busy man. We picked up more mail
and brought home more pictures of Pete!

As a way of thanking us, Pete secured field seats for
all three stadiums out West for us. It was a delightful
road trip that we shared with the Reds.

7

The Rookie

When Pete became a member of the Cincinnati Reds in 1963, Fred Hutchinson was the manager. Hutch started out in the majors in 1939 with Detroit, and except for service in World War II, he was with the team till 1953.

The Reds still consisted of most of the players that had taken them to the World Series in 1961. Besides Pinson and Maloney, they had Gordy Coleman, Frank Robinson, Johnny Edwards, Gene Freese, Leo Cardenas, Tommy Harper, Eddie Kasko, Don Pavletich, Marty Keough, and Daryl Spencer. For pitchers they had Jim O'Toole, Joe Nuxhall, John Tsitouris, Joey Jay, Bob Purkey, and Al Worthington. And they had, for better or for worse, Peter Edward Rose.

The previous year the Minnesota Twins' Harmon Killebrew led the American League in homers with 45; Milwaukee Braves' outfielder Hank Aaron led the National with 44. Vada Pinson of the Reds had 204 hits to lead the league, and Reds' fireballer Jim Maloney was the master of National League hitters with a pitching percentage of .767, with 23 wins, 265 strikeouts, and 6 shutouts.

In 1962 the Reds had won 98 and lost 64. Robinson was coming off a .342 season; Pinson, .292; and Cardenas, .294. And amid these mighty diamond heroes stepped the rookie second baseman from the hometown. The kid had talent. But was it a publicity stunt by the Reds or did he really have a future in the Majors?

The Rose clan was there, of course, and lots of pictures were taken to commemorate the event. Pete was nervous; Harry Rose was nervous; but Pete's mom? Like a rock!

Then umpire Jocko Conlan shouted, "Play ball!"

The Cincinnati Redlegs were the first professional baseball team, founded in 1869 as a barnstorming outfit, taking on all comers for a price. More than any other team, they had tradition, and recognizing that hallowed history, the Major League powers that be give the Reds the honor of hosting the first game of every season.

Opening days in Cincinnati are holidays. Everything comes to a stop but the traffic lights. But that opening day of 1963 marked an historic occasion because Pete Rose was playing his first Major League game.

The Reds were playing the Pittsburgh Pirates, and Earl Francis was pitching for them. He had finished 1962 with a 9-8 record and an ERA of 3.07. The Pirates had finished fourth in 1962, a game behind the Reds.

When Pete came to bat the fans cheered. He stood there, facing Francis, the six-foot two, 210-pound

Pittsburgh pitcher, who had been in the majors the two years Pete had been traveling around the minors.

First pitch — ball.

But as he had done ever since playing in the Knot Hole circuit as a kid in Cincinnati, Pete followed the ball from the moment it left the pitcher's hand until it plopped into the catcher's glove.

Jocko Conlan, the plate umpire, had never seen Pete play before, so he took offense at Pete looking back. Jocko growled, "Listen, you young rookie, don't look back here at me. I don't need no help with my calls."

Pete said nothing, being too scared to do anything with 30,000 fans there in the stands, watching.

Next pitch — ball two!

Pete watched it all the way into the catcher's mitt, but this time Conlan said nothing. Merely glared.

The third pitch was the same.

Jocko Conlan was no dummy. He soon understood that Pete wasn't trying to show him up and realized that it was Pete's way of hitting; watching the ball from the moment it leaves the pitcher's hand until he either swings at it or it reaches the catcher's mitt.

Francis hurled again and — ball four!

Pete dropped the bat and ran down the first base line as fast he could. That was his style — the hustling play taught to him by his father — and the fans loved it. Pete had a walk in his first appearance at the plate for the Cincinnati Reds. Before the inning was over, he had his first run scored, too, coming home on a homerun by Frank Robinson.

The game continued. The Reds won. And Pete? He

went hitless in three official trips and committed his first big league error on a ground ball off the bat of Bob Skinner. Pete had his baptism under fire. No homerun on first trip to the plate; not even a single. Nothing terribly dramatic occured. He was just another rookie that didn't exactly strike terror in the hearts of opposing pitchers.

But he was a Major League rookie, and that was all that counted. Pete Rose had arrived, and as the year wore on, everyone found out how he had arrived.

Three games later Pete did get that first hit of his major league career. "The Warrior", Bob Friend, was on the mound for the Pirates. Friend was once considered the ace of the Pittsburgh staff, and although he had been in the league since 1951, he could still hum it in there. Fastball! Pete, hitting lefthanded, got it solidly on the bat, and a screaming liner found the gap in leftfield. Down to first, the turn for second, past second — the throw was coming in — a head first slide into third, and — "Safe!" yelled the umpire. Pete jumped up and dusted himself off, and the official scorekeeper circled *3B* in the scorebook. Pete Rose had a triple for the first hit of a career that would eclipse three decades and see him break records aplenty.

But that was in Cincinnati. Before the hometown crowd. What about the other ball parks throughout the National League. How would Pete hit on the road? Would he play in front of crowds that would cheer him or boo him or what?

For Pete, going on the road for the first time was a real experience, one he had only dreamed about before.

Each new city was exciting for him, another dream come true. The first thing he would do was go out and stare at each ball park.

The National League had 10 teams in 1963: Chicago, Cincinnati, Houston, Los Angeles, Milwaukee, New York, Philadelphia, Pittsburgh, St. Louis, and San Francisco. The New York Mets and Houston Astros (nee Colt .45s) were expansion teams, added to the league in 1962. Houston began their history by shellacking the hapless Chicago Cubs, and those "Amazin' Mets" of New York started off like the so-called Bums of Brooklyn used to play by losing their first nine games.

Of the 10 teams, only two, San Francisco and Los Angeles, had new ball parks. All the other teams were playing on fields built long before World War II, some even earlier than World War I, such as Wrigley Field in Chicago.

The Mets played in the old Polo Grounds; the same field where Willie Mays made that amazing over the shoulder catch of a Vic Wertz drive in the 1954 World Series between the then New York Giants and the Cleveland Indians; the same field where Bobby Thomson's two-out, ninth inning homer propelled the Giants past the Dodgers in the third game of their three-game playoff for the National League Pennant and into the 1951 World Series against the crosstown Yankees. Pete had read how Mel Ott used to cock his leg, then go downtown with the long ball. Christie Mathewson used to "mow 'em down" from the same mound that Mets' pitchers were using to throw fastballs at Pete.

And St. Louis was still in the old Sportsman's Park. "Stan the Man" Musial rounded the bases there more than a few times, and the "Gashouse Gang" of the 1930s roared to victory behind the great pitching of Dizzy and Paul Dean.

When Pete was a boy, he used to read about Ralph Kiner's explosive homers in old Forbes Field. Only two years before Pete made it to the Big Time Bill Mazeroski belted a lead-off round-tripper in the bottom of the ninth to make winners of the Pirates over the Yankees in the 1961 World Series.

Philadelphia has always been a good baseball town, although the Phillies haven't always been the best of teams. The 1950 "Whiz Kids" won the pennant, then had to face the Yankees in the Series, only to lose in four straight. Grover Cleveland Alexander, "Alex the Great", toiled in Philly for more than a few seasons.

Milwaukee's County Stadium was a fairly new park back then, being the home of the Braves since they moved there in 1953. But even so, it had its moments in baseball history. Hank Aaron, Eddie Mathews, Joe Adcock, Johnny Logan, Billy Bruton, Andy Pafko, Del Crandall, Warren Spahn, Lew Burdette, and Bob Buhl had sparked the Braves to pennants in 1957 and 1958 and almost made it three in a row in 1959 before losing in a playoff to the Los Angeles Dodgers. They also achieved one of the rare feats of World Series history when they came back from a 3-1 deficit to beat the Yankees in the 1957 annual fall classic.

Houston didn't have the Astrodome yet, just the old park, where a lot of night games were played because it was too hot to play day games. The players called it "Mosquitoville" because millions of mosquitoes infested the park night after night, annoying the players and the fans.

Then there was Chicago. Of all the baseball arenas in the history of the game, maybe none has seen as much history as beautiful Wrigley Field, the home of the Cubs since the second decade of this century. No night baseball on Chicago's North Side, just day games. And that fact has played its part in history, like the last game of the 1938 season when Gabby Hartnett hit his "homer in the gloaming" to win the pennant for the Cubs. Hack Wilson set one National League and one Major League record while playing for the Cubs when he hit 56 homeruns and drove in 190 runs. And visiting ballplayers have had their days at Wrigley too, like when Babe Ruth pointed to the stands and indicated where he was about to park a four-bagger in a World Series game. Yes, those famed ivy-covered walls of Wrigley Field have witnessed a lot of history, and Pete has added to it for over 20 years.

Of those parks being used in 1963, Pete liked some of them then, and he still likes them now. But there are those that he still dislikes. His least favorite is San Francisco's Candlestick Park. "It's cold out there. The place holds 42,500 and I'll bet you lots of times they're all huddled together trying to get warm, and wishing the fog would go away. San Francisco is a pretty town but it sure is a damp and chilly place to play baseball, which I personally like to consider a hot-weather game. Also, Candlestick Park has a rough

Dear Pete   83

infield. Don't forget that."

Pete's favorite ballpark? Chicago. Why? Says Pete, "When those bleacher bums in Wrigley Field get on me, they forget one thing. That kind of stuff only makes me work harder. So, in reality, they aren't getting my goat. They're getting the best I got in me. The worst thing that crowd ever threw at me was a crutch, a legitimate crutch! Listen, I was playing there one day when they had to call the game for a few minutes so the groundskeepers could clear off the field. They had thrown everything my way. They had thrown those paper cups for beer, popcorn boxes, hot dogs, fish, and even chicken bones. When they got through throwing stuff my way the field looked like an incinerator. I got the biggest kick out of those characters in the Wrigley Field bleachers. I can't get mad at them. How can I? They take their baseball as seriously as I take my baseball which make them, whether they want to be or not, my kind of people."

Dodger Stadium in Los Angeles is second to Chicago as the best place to play away games, according to Pete. For a newer park, he considers it to be the most beautiful.

Pete likes Philadelphia because of the fans. He rates Philly fans among the most knowledgeable and passionate. They have a reputation of being hard on their hometown players, but that's because they expect each player to be giving back to the game everything he's taking out of it. That's the way Pete plays and he feels other players should play with the same enthusiasm and desire to give the fans what they pay to see.

Houston is a great place to play, in Pete's book, for two reasons: the fans and the Astrodome. The Texas fans are very rabid baseball watchers, and they add an excitement to the game with their yells and hoots. And the Astrodome, the first domed stadium anywhere in the world, although it means playing baseball indoors when it was meant to be played outdoors, gives every game there ideal weather conditions for playing the game.

Jack Murphy Stadium in San Diego is Pete's idea of the prettiest park of all. And he likes the Cardinals' park in St. Louis because it's made for hitters like he is.

Pittsburgh's Three Rivers Stadium and Cincinnati's Riverfront Stadium are okay as new parks go. Their artificial surfaces are good for hitters like Pete, and the fences aren't too deep like in St. Louis for the power strokers.

Atlanta's Fulton County Stadium and Shea Stadium in New York are nice parks, but they are primarily advantageous to the long-ballers. Pete likes Atlanta because it's always warm there.

The only two that really bother him are Candlestick Park in San Francisco and Olympic Stadium in Montreal. But it's not the parks that disturb him; it's the weather. Maybe that explains why Pete didn't fair as well in Montreal when he played for the Expos for part of 1984. Montreal is simply too cold for baseball, and so is San Francisco. Houston has a domed stadium because it's too hot there, so Pete feels San Francisco and Montreal should have domed stadiums because their weather is too cold.

The Polo Grounds in New York had atmosphere and history going for it when the Mets entered the league in 1962, but Pete wasn't sorry to see the move to the new stadium in Flushing Meadows. Baseball games weren't meant to be won or lost on pop-up homers down the line by hitters who can't hit their own weight.

Of all the old stadiums, and this has to be taken with a grain of salt considering where Pete is from, Pete preferred Crosley Field in Cincinnati. The fences were long enough all the way around to keep the cheapie homers in the park but short enough to let legitimate wallops get out. And the terraced outfield added the kind of excitement to every game played there that baseball was meant to have. For the fan, there was nothing like watching Vada Pinson race back in centerfield, climbing the terrace with every step, to haul down a long drive that would have been over his head and maybe off the wall in most other parks. Crosley Field gave the Reds that real home field advantage that baseball teams are supposed to have.

Riverfront Stadium isn't much different than most of the other new parks around with its symmetrical layout. There is nothing about it that really separates it from Philadelphia's field or Pittsburgh's, New York's, Atlanta's, LA's, Houston's, St. Louis', Montreal's, San Diego's or San Francisco's, all of which have stadiums built in the last three decades and all of which have symmetrical designs. It can be argued that Wrigley Field in Chicago has a symmetrical design, but the fact that the walls bend in at the power alleys give it a distinction no other field has.

The new parks were necessary for the sake of the fans in one respect. They gave everyone a clear view of the play on the field, and the seating was more comfortable. On the other hand, they took away some of the color of the game and some of the advantage for the home team. One good example of the home field advantage still around is Boston's Fenway Park. The "Green Monster" in leftfield allows the Red Sox to load up their lineup with righthanded power hitters, and it makes left-handed pitchers weep. Yankee Stadium in New York is still something of a lefthanded hitters paradise, al-though recent renovations have taken away some of that. How good would Babe Ruth, Lou Gehrig, and Roger Maris have been if they had played their careers in Boston? And how much greater would Ted Williams have been if he'd played in Yankee Stadium his whole career?

Yes, the home field used to be a real advantage for every team that depended on power to win games, but not anymore. Now the advantage goes to teams with hitters like Pete Rose, hitters who stroke liners in the gaps for extra bases, hitters who slap hard grounders into the hole off artificial turf and get a solid single, hitters who are expert at the art of bunting and drag a dinker between the pitcher and first base and beat the throw for a hit.

Pete began his career at time when baseball was changing from a game of brute force to one that re-quired greater skill with the bat and above all more hustle. No longer do teams put slow overweight slug-gers in the outfield. Now they have fleet-footed speedsters who have to race after every ball hit to the outfield, especially those hit between the fielders because a drive into the gap can get past them quicker off the artificial turf. No longer can they put a poor fielding homerun hitter on first base to keep him in the lineup. Artificial turf changed that too.

And Pete helped cause these changes with his style of play. His hustling, his all-out performance on every pitch, led other players to follow his example or have short careers in the Big Leagues.

When Pete joined the Reds for good in 1963, baseball was in the midst of a metamorphosis, and Pete Rose was the one man who did more to change the game than any other.

As he travelled around the league that first year of his career, Pete saw sights, heard sounds, and viewed people he may never have otherwise seen without a career in baseball. Each city was a new adventure for him. New York, the Big Apple; Chicago, the Windy City; Los Angeles, the City of Angels; Philadelphia, the City of Brotherly Love.

Here's how Pete described his first trip to New York. "My first trip to New York City impressed me. They had us down there in the Hotel Roosevelt, which is a long way from the park so we'd go to the park by chartered bus. I saw more bridges than any city ought to have. And I'd spend the whole bus ride with my nose pressed against the window, gawking out at the people. Listen, some of them were real freaks. They wouldn't have lasted ten seconds in Sedamsville. We used to go through Harlem on the way to the Polo Grounds and that always struck me as kind of sad. Seems like there was nothing but acres and acres of tenements, each one in worse shape than the others. We'd yell at the people and they'd yell back at us. Nothing mean. Nobody was mad at anyone. And I remember one time we were traveling through some pretty ritzy neighborhood where we had seen people walking their dogs and cats on a leash, only there was this one guy and on his leash was a duck! Yeah, New York is a lot different than Sedamsville."

Back then, Pete only took two suits with him for a ten-day road trip. Times have changed, and so has Pete's salary. He only had two suits back then. Now he takes along a whole closet.

His first roommate on the road was Daryl Spencer, who had come to Cincinnati by way of Los Angeles, St. Louis, San Francisco, and New York. Spencer was an older player with plenty of baseball savvy. Pete suspected that Manager Hutchinson put Pete in with Spencer because of his knowledge of the game, hoping some of it would rub off on Pete. They would sit around the hotel rooms on the road and talk nothing but baseball.

And when that wasn't happening in a place like New York, Pete would go down to the train station during rush hour and watch all the bodies go by, the commuter crowds. Or he would visit the sights, like the Empire State Building.

Chicago has its attractions, or distractions, depending on how you look at them. Pete would go the movies there quite a bit in those early years. But he didn't habituate the bars because he's not a drinker. He did pay a visit or two to Chicago's notorious Rush Street back then, and he recalled seeing a Greek belly dancer once. His comment about her was, "She would have made a dandy shortstop."

Pete's first road game was in Philadelphia. Art Mahaffey, who had gone to Western Hills High School long before Pete had, was pitching for the Phillies. He had been there since 1960, and in 1962 he had won 19 and lost 14, including 1 shutout. On the chilly day Pete faced him, Mahaffey was hot and much to Pete's chagrin struck out Pete four straight times. That was not one of Pete's most cherished games, but it was a memorable one. How often did he get struck out four times in 32 degree weather?

Baseball players talk to each other on the field as well as off, and sometimes this can be hazardous to a man's play. And older, more experienced players will talk to rookies on the field incessantly sometimes in an effort to make them make a mistake that just might turn a game around, especially if that rookie is on the other team.

Pete put up with a lot of that his first year, but it didn't take long before opposing players found out he was smarter than most rookies. But Pete did have his bad moments.

For instance, there was the time right after Pete had gotten a traffic ticket in Newport, Kentucky and he was up to bat when the opposing catcher asked him, "Hey, Pete, what were you really doing over there?"

"Nothing," said Pete — and zip, there would go the

ball.

"Are you sure?"

"I wasn't doing anything over there."

Zip! There went the ball again.

It's a little embarrassing to let two straight perfect strikes go by.

Pete also remembers a catcher-batter conversation he had once with Philadelphia backstopper Mike Ryan.

"Now, Pete, I'm going to tell you what's coming next."

Pete ignored him.

"Here comes a fast ball," said Ryan. "Here comes a fast ball!"

And sure enough, there came a fast ball.

Pete said, "Aw, shut up, man. I don't want to know what's coming."

"Here comes a curve."

Sure enough. It was a curve.

"Listen," Pete complained to plate umpire Doug Harvey, "can you shut this guy up?"

"Not me," said the umpire. "I can't shut him up."

"Here comes another fast ball."

And it was.

That little gambit worked the first two times Pete came to bat that game, but the third trip to the plate was different. Ryan called the pitch, and Pete believed him, cracking a double and driving in a man from second.

The next day Ryan wasn't calling any more pitches.

Maury Wills of the Dodgers almost caught Pete off base, so to speak, but also literally. After making a head-first slide into second, Pete stood up to dust himself off, and Wills said, "Excuse me, Pete. I'm going to kick off the bag." Some rookies would do the polite thing and step off, only to be tagged out. But not Pete. He held his ground.

When Pete's first season was over, he had played in 157 games with 623 official trips to the plate. His statistics showed a batting average of .273 with 170 hits, 25 doubles, 9 triples, and 6 homeruns. Not too bad. He also had 72 strikeouts and 55 walks, and he stole 13 bases, all on hustle because he was no Lou Brock or Maury Wills.

Opposing pitchers booked Pete as a good curveball hitter, so they were always trying to jam him with one. He faced some of the greatest lefthanders in the history of baseball that year, and those men had one of the great seasons of their careers, too. Among them were Sandy Koufax, who ended the 1963 season with a winning percentage of .833; Warren Spahn in Milwaukee, who finished with a winning percentage of .767; and Ron Perranoski of the Dodgers, who led the league with his winning percentage of .842 (he won 16 and lost 3). On the righthanded side were guys like Juan Marichal, who hailed from the Dominican Republic and who had a winning percentage that year of .758 for San Francisco.

The Reds ended in fifth place, 86-76, 13 games behind Los Angeles. "Wait till next year," was the cry.

The next year— 1964 — would be Pete's sophomore year in the majors. And, if you remember how he messed up the tenth grade at Western Hills High School, you know what a lousy sophomore he made.

8

For the Fans

As I said before, my husband Tony and I have been Reds fans for years, so we've known Pete for a long time. Except for his mother, we may know him better than anyone. He's like family to us, and like our own children, we love him for what he is.

Pete's no perfect angel, but who is? He's had his ups and downs, and he's made his share of mistakes in this world. That only proves he's human after all.

But he loves baseball, and he loves baseball fans. He'll do almost anything for the game and for its fans. He's that kind of guy.

It's been my hope that the fans who read this book understand this and get to be better fans of the game, the same as Pete is. I know that I've learned to appreciate other fans more since being his Fan Mail Secretary, and I'm hoping that by sharing his mail with you that you will, too.

Dear Mr. Rose,

I wrote you a letter a few months ago asking for your autograph on a baseball card. I just wanted to write to you again and thank you for doing it. And also to say that the next time you come down around Jacksonville (Fla.) stop by and we'll talk some and pass some baseball.

A big fan of you and the Reds,
David

A thank you for an autograph. I'm sure Pete would enjoy "passing" some baseballs with you.

Dear Pete:

I don't like the way you are being treated because if anyone deserves all he can get it is you.

You have given 110% for years and the fans love you for it. I guess I'm as loyal a redleg fan as anyone and love the whole team, but I can't imangine the Reds without Pete Rose. Please don't ever leave us Pete, can't stand to think of you in any other uniform. Hope every thing works out right for you, we need you.

Sincerely,
Mrs. Richard P.

I had the opportunity to read some of Pete's earlier mail. He had problems with management on contract negotiations several times in the past. No one in baseball plays as hard as Pete Rose; he does give 110% all the time.

Dear Mr. Rose,

*Some while back you very kindly responded to the request of
our grandson, Mark for your autograph.*

*I thought you would enjoy hearing that Mark's mom,
"caught him off base telling his friends he could look at the
signature for a $1.00! And to help the cuse, I've added to his
treasure a Pete Rose glass from King Kurk and an autographed baseball offered by General Foods.*

We're all Pete Rose and Reds fans.

*Thank you for the autograph and best of luck to you and the
Team.*

Sincerely,

Margaret

This was one enterprising lad! One dollar to see an
autograph? Now let me see, where shall I begin? (Only
kidding.)

Dear Mr. Rose,

*I wanted to write to you and express my best wishes to you on
your fabulous accomplishments that you have obtained during
your great career. Although I am an avid St. Louis Cardinal
fan I really respect you and your Big Red Machine because
they are super. I guess sometime in the 1978 baseball season
you will get your 3,000th hit and that will have been one feat
that I know will please you. I really admire you for your hussle
and dedication to your profession. You are a true professional
in every sense of the word. For years, I have likend you to Ty
Cobb because you both gave it all you had all the time, you both
loved to win and hated to lose. One thing else is that you both
weren't to popular outside your own city. But I don't under-*

stand it. You have to be one of the best players to ever play this great game of Baseball. I know how you feel about baseball because I love it to and can't live without it. Baseball is the most exciting game there is and you make it that way Pete. You have a beautiful family. Just remember that when you come to St. Louis you always have one fan who really respects you as a ball player and as a person. Just thank you alot for all the pleasure and baseball history that you have given me and may your goals that you have set all be accomplished.

   Janet

This great fan has said it all. Pete is a dedicated ballplayer. He had his 3,000th hit in '78 and his 4,000th hit in '84. At that rate, he'll get his 5,000th hit in 1990, and don't think he won't try.

Dear Pete Rose,

   Could you send me 3 box seat tickets? I would like two other things. A book with very good batting tips in it and a catcher's mit. Thanks. good luck this year.

   Sincerely,

   James

This youngster has Pete mixed up with Santa Claus.

Dear Pete Rose,

   Thanks alot for your (the whole Cincinnati Reds) work in 1975 and 1976. Billy Martin (Yankee Manager) wants to get another crack at the Reds in the Series. Well, he just can't accept that the Reds were more superior to the Yanks. I can't stand Martin because he said, "I'd like to stick Pete Rose's ugly

96   **Dear Pete**

face in the mud." 1) His (Martin's) face isn't so pretty, 2) Your not ugly.

I'm in the 7th grade in school. My friends all like the Reds.

My mom told me to say in my letter to you that her and my dad graduated from Western Hills High School (what years I don't know) too bad about the years they graduated in because then I might be able to figure out how old she is. (She says she's 29, but you know how moms are sometimes).

In early March I signed up for Little League. I'd like some advice. First, how do you field a line drive hit directly at you? Second, sometimes I get scared when I'm at bat. Sound strange huh? Maybe I'd just better go to the funny farm.

Last but not least, could I also have your autograph? (you've heard it before)

Chow,
   Miss Laurie

Laurie, you are so right, Pete is not ugly! I know there are some people who will differ with me, but Pete is a good looking gentleman.

Dear Mr. Rose:

Perhaps this is the most unusual request you have ever received, or perhaps you receive many similar ones. However, this is the first time I have ever done anything like this.

I am writing about my grand-daughter who lives in Massachusetts. She is an avid sports fan and her team is the Cincinnati Reds — guess who her hero is. None other than Pete Rose. Her 14 year old brother is just as keen on sports but his team is the Red Sox so they have a great time together watching the games. Incidentally, Elaine is 16 today but she doesn't

Dear Pete   **97**

know I am writing to you.

She has a picture of you that she cut from some magazine and she carries it with her when she comes to visit us. It goes on her wall in the room where she sleeps. The thing that got me was when she was saying her prayers each night she always said "God bless Pete Rose" I thought I bet he doesn't know there is a little girl praying for him each night even though she has never seen him in person.

Her father was a great sports fan too (The Yankees) but unfortunately he died before she was four and her brother was two — the two of them are great pals even though they differ on teams.

Would it be asking too much if you would send her a Christmas card? It would make her the happiest girl in the world. If you would I would be eternally grateful. Thanks and a very Merry Christmas to you and yours,

    Mary

An autographed picture was sent to Elaine. I bet she and her brother have great fun rooting for their favorite teams. A great problem would exist when both teams play on T.V. at the same time. A big hug to such a thoughtful grandmother writing for Pete's picture for a granddaughter.

Mr. Rose,

Congratulations on your past World Series. Since I was about 5 years old I had always followed the Reds. You have been my inspiration through high school and college ball. I am presently a freshman at R.J.C. where in 1973 they won nationals. I am presently on the J.V.'s, but plan to work my way up. I have been an infielder, 2nd base as a matter of fact and they moved me to the outfield where I'm starting with a .333 average I remember reading a book where the same occured to you. It's a lot more comfortable. I have also picked up your style of running over people that tend to get in the way. I'm 5'7" and weigh 160, but it's fun.

I'd really appreciate it if you could send a signed picture of you running over somebody. I'd give anything to have even your autographed picture, cause you have truly been my inspiration through baseball's ups and downs. If possible could you have it mailed to my home at this address. It would really mean an awful lot to me.

Yours truly

David

P.S. Is there an easier way to write to you. I mean is it possible for me to write you at a home address I'd like to keep in touch, since it is often very boring over here.

I'm afraid Pete's pictures are not the type that show him running over people. The newspapers may have some of this type of photo and one can have a duplicate made for a price. I sent an autographed picture of Pete. I hope it sufficed.

Dear Mr. Rose —

I wonder if you would be kind enough to send me a signed picture of yourself. The one we have is a newspaper clipping two years old and quite faded. We would like it for part of our boy's Christmas.

He is 18 years old and a Mongoloid child. To him, you are Pete "Wose".

Dear Pete   **99**

Perhaps you have seen us at the games in Tampa. We were sitting to the right of that loud mouth your brother went after last year. We were so busy getting our boy out of his aisle seat, (didn't want to take a chance on a stray punch) that we missed most of the excitement.

Anyhow, I am enclosing a picture. His name is Tommy.

Thank you very much if this can be done this time of year.

See you this spring.

Sincerely,

Alice L.

I was surprised when I saw the address on the letter, that of a motel. We stayed at it one time in Tampa. Tommy is a nice lad, so are his parents. The autographed picture was sent, and I know it made a young boy very happy.

Dear Pete,

I am 16 years old and a big fan of yours. I watch all of the Reds games.

The reason I'm writing you is because, first of all, I would like to have a picture of you signed to me.

The other reason is because, you see I play Girls softball, for New Castle. Our games are over now of course. Someday I would like to play for the Reds. Anyway the reason I'm writing is because I play 3rd base and I slide like you do. Everytime I slide I get scabbed up knees. I need you help fast before I ruin my knees. "Please help me Pete!"

Hope you write back soon.

A big fan of yours

Terri

This young lady needs knee pads to help cushion her when she slides. I wonder when the major leagues will have a female player? I am sure one will make it some day. Females are into auto racing, horse racing, golf, tennis, so why not baseball?

Dear Mr. Pete Rose,

I realize that you have about ten times as many fans as you do hits, but out of them all I consider myself your No. 1 fan.

I am seventeen years old and ever since I've known about baseball you have been my idol. Since I am a girl I haven't been able to participate in baseball, but softball has been my game for four years now.

The reason I am writing this letter is because I want to meet you and perhaps your family. Next to my career ambitions, my greatest ambition is to meet you — Pete Rose — Charlie Hustle. Like I said you do have alot of fans, but I feel out of all of them I am No. 1.

I have a positive attitude about meeting you next to all the discouraging words I get from my friends. So, please answer my letter with a positive answer.

I want to visit Cincinnati — Home of the World Champions and while visiting, I hope to meet you and your family.

Please answer this letter telling me it will be possible in the near future to meet you.

I am looking forward to hearing from you.

Your No. 1 fan!

Mary S.

Many fans want to meet Pete and his family. Setting a definite date is impossible. Pete has had requests from people wanting to take a tour of his home. Can you imagine the confusion, people coming in and out and Pete's family trying to live a normal life.

A public figure has very little privacy. Several of the players we know have told us how perfect strangers ring their doorbells, asking for an autograph, even at dinner time.

Dear Pete:

I just wanted to tell you how you inspired and helped a little Mongoloid boy who is eight years old and a great baseball fan. He is my great grandson and lives with his grandparents.

Brian is handicapped by being mongoloid and he cannot talk. He has been taking speech therapy and each week he is given a few words to try to say. Last week one of the words was "Ball". He was visiting at my home and watching television as usual, when the commercial, showing you in the baseball uniform of the Reds and right out of a clear sky Brian said, "Ball". He had connected you with the word because he knew you were a ball player — (and a great one at that). We were so happy to hear him say one of his words that I just had to write and tell you about it as I thought perhaps you might get a kick out of it.

Brian will be watching for you so keep up the good work Pete.

Best of Luck
Sincerely
Doris H.

Pete was thrilled that Brian associated him with the word "ball."

Dear Mr. Rose,

I would like to thank you for the way yo were so nice to Greg the other day when you made the commercial for the Hearing and Speech Impaired Children around the world. It is so nice when someone takes just a few minutes with a child like this. So we, Greg's parents and his brothers, would like to say thanks to you for Greg. Maybe one day with the help from people like you and clubs like this our little Greg will be able to come to you and say thank you himself.

I would like to thank you for the shirt and the ball you sign for him. He liked them very much. He would wear the shirt around the clock if I let him. Greg goes through the paper every evening to see if he can find your picture. Maybe Greg will get to see his first ball game this summer at Riverfront since he will be five on the 4th of July.

Thank you again for your kindness and help.

  Mrs. Nicholas

  (Greg's mother)

P.S. With a little coaching we have Greg saying "Pete" and a little sound is great to us. "Thank you again".

I think that says it all.

9

Sophomore to Seasoned Veteran

The end of the season in 1963 to the end of the 1964 campaign was a year that Pete would like to forget.

It was the year he did his military training; the year he suffered the infamous "Sophomore Jinx" that many players who have outstanding rookie seasons endure; the year a great guy, Fred Hutchinson, died.

Sandy Koufax struck out 15 Yankees to set a new World Series record, and the Los Angeles Dodgers clipped the Bronx Bombers in four straight games to win the World Series in 1963. President John F. Kennedy was assassinated in Dallas on November 22, and Lyndon Baines Johnson became the first president from Texas. The Warren Commission determined the murder was done by Lee Harvery Oswald alone. More astronauts and cosmonauts circled the globe in outer space, and the Philadelphia Phillies led the National League from the beginning of the season right up into September, only to fold in the last two weeks of the season and finish in a tie for second place with the Reds, only one game behind the St. Louis Cardinals.

The only true bright spot during the year as far as Pete's baseball career was concerned was the fact that he was voted National League Rookie-of-the-Year for 1963. His stats for the year were: 170 hits, 26 doubles, 9 triples, 6 homers, 41 RBIs, 13 stolen bases, and 101 runs scored. His batting average was .273 in 157 games. He garnered 17 of the 20 votes, with two going to Mets' second-sacker Ron Hunt and the other going to Phillies' pitcher Ray Culp.

Pete did his military training at Fort Knox, Kentucky, and he was none the worse for it. The experience only added a little color to his life, and it gave him a few insights into the ways of leadership that have carried over to his new managerial status with the Reds. He went off to Fort Knox right after the end of the 1963 season as a member of the Ohio National Guard, and he was free again by the time spring training came around in February.

This was also the year Pete gave up bachelorhood. While the other recruits were running into Louisville on passes, Pete made tracks for Cincinnati. Why? Love. Karolyn Ann Engelhardt became Mrs. Peter Edward Rose on January 25, 1964, one week after Pete finished basic training. They spent their honeymoon in a small motel near Fort Knox.

After basic training Pete was assigned to a reserve engineering unit that was stationed in Fort Thomas, Kentucky, right across the river from Cincinnati. This was convenient, of course, because it allowed Pete to be near the Reds during the season.

The only bad experience that came out of that time was when Pete was interviewed by a reporter while they stood near a Coke machine. Pete joked that life in the military was really tough, so tough that he was really there to guard the machine. The trouble was the reporter took him seriously, or so it seemed when the interview reached print. Pete got a lot of lousy mail over that one.

Spring training time came, and Pete was off to Florida. He was a very happy young man when he arrived in Tampa, but Earl Lawson of the *Cincinnati Post* brought an unsavory fact to Pete's attention. Some — not many, but a few — of the white guys on the team resented Pete because of his friendship with black players. Those players didn't want much to do with Pete, but Pete didn't care a whole lot because Frank Robinson and Vada Pinson treated him like a real brother.

Pete pointed up this fact. "One night when we were playing in Chicago and I had got to the hotel ten minutes after the midnight curfew and my roommate at the time had locked our door and I knocked on it but he wouldn't open it so there I stood in the hall, wondering what to do. Eventually I went upstairs to where Vada Pinson was, he opened the door, and he said, 'Come on, Pete. You can sleep in here.' Robinson, his regular roommate, was back in Cincinnati, getting his arm worked on. But that's the way the guys were to me. Most of them, as you can see, were swell. The ones who weren't — well, that's water over the dam."

The Reds opened the 1964 season unaware of the

dark secret Fred Hutchinson was carrying. He had terminal cancer. It would be his last campaign, one he would wage bravely though his body was continually racked with pain. He never let on to his players that he was dying.

Pete felt his sophomore year was not too spectacular considering his status as Rookie-of-the-Year. It was his opinion that the old "Sophomore Jinx" caught up with him. His batting average dropping a mere four points to .269 was hardly a bad year.

The Reds were a better team in 1964, coming in second to the St. Louis Cardinals in one of the Game's wildest finishes ever. With two-plus weeks left, the Phillies appeared to have the pennant all wrapped up when the strangest thing happened. The league leaders since the first week of the season lost 10 straight, and the Reds and Cardinals turned it on. Entering the final weekend of the season, it was anyone's guess who would win the flag. The Cards finally took it on the last day of the season.

Pete appeared in only 136 games, the least amount of games played by him in a season when he wasn't injured or there wasn't a players strike. He spent a lot of time on the bench. He failed to start in 37 games, being used as a pinch-hitter 11 times and getting only two hits.

To say Pete was unhappy is an understatement. But he took it like the man he is. He knew it was no one's fault but his own. If you don't produce, you don't play.

Pete may have been angry with himself, but he wasn't discouraged to the point of giving up or even thinking of giving up. And neither were his friends and family.

Joe and Beatrice Lask and their four children made a sign and hung it on the bleacher wall. It read: "ROSE CAN'T BLOOM ON A BENCH!" It was just the kind of encouragement Pete needed.

But there he was on the bench. So Pete took his hitting woes to the team batting coach, Ted Kluszewski. "Big Klu" was no slouch as a hitter, whether for power or average. He had a life-time BA of .298, and he got his share of homers, banging out 40 in 1953, 49 in 1954, and 47 in 1955. He played 11 years with the Reds from 1947 to 1957, before being traded to Pittsburgh. He then moved to Chicago in late August 1959 and helped the White Sox to the American League pennant. When his playing career was over he returned to the Reds as their hitting instructor.

Pete did four things to break his batting slump. He tried using a heavier bat, then a lighter one. Then he tried moving up higher in the batter's box, then back in the box. But he never changed his stance. The first two years in the majors he used the thickest-handled bat there was. It's called a U-1. He also choked up those years. Then "Big Klu" said if he used a skinny-handled bat, he'd be able to pull the ball better and it was to Pete's advantage to pull the ball because otherwise the opposition will just play him to hit to left field when he bats left-handed. It is a big advantage to hit to all three fields, and once Pete learned that trick he was on his way to a career paralleled by few.

But by the time Pete was in the groove again and back in the starting lineup, the season was over. So he asked if he could play winter ball, and the front office said yes. So Pete boned up on Spanish and boarded a plane for Caracas, Venezuela.

He went to South America with Reds coach Reggie Otero. It was during a weekend series in Santo Domingo, The Dominican Republic, that Pete and Reggie heard of Fred Hutchinson's death. They were riding a bus that had a radio on, and a newscaster reported Hutchinson's demise in Spanish. Pete only caught the name of his late manager. But Reggie understood every word, and he began crying at the sad news. Not because his best friend was dead, but because he was in the Dominican Republic and couldn't go to the funeral.

Pete was remorseful, too, but for a different reason. "The Bear", as Hutchinson was fondly called by those who knew him well, had been a father-figure to Pete. More than that, Hutch was the man who had placed his confidence in Pete and brought him to the Major Leagues. Pete has always felt robbed because he never got to hit .300 for Hutch.

The main reason Pete was in Venezuela was to improve his play, but the money wasn't bad either. For a guy like Pete, other winter jobs might have been more lucrative but not nearly as much fun.

Otero was down there for one reason: coach Pete. And Pete learned. He hit a solid .340 and led the four-team circuit in runs scored. His Caracas team (there were two) won the championship.

Helping Otero was Alex Carrasquel, a native of Venezuela who had pitched for the old Washington

Senators (the ones who became the Minnesota Twins in 1960) in the 1940s. He would keep Pete after games to hit him ground balls, an art Pete felt he needed to learn a lot better, especially after his first game in the winter league when he committed four errors in one inning and felt so bad he nearly walked off the field to go back to the States.

Tommy Helms was also in Venezuela but on another team in Caracas that shared the stadium Pete's team used. They roomed together until their wives came down. Helms was there to learn his position better and to improve his hitting. To date, he had had only one official trip to the plate in a Reds uniform. Tommy, from North Carolina, and Pete hung around together, both being *norteamericanos* and both from the Cincinnati *Rojas*. They would watch each other play when one had a day off and the other was on the field.

Pete stayed in Venezuela the whole winter except for the weekend trip to Santo Domingo and a trip home for Christmas. Then it was February and spring training in Tampa.

Most players who play winter ball have an edge over those who don't when spring training starts. Pete certainly felt that way in 1965, but he didn't show too much just the same until the season started.

Pete had good stats in '65, numbers that soon became rather routine for him. He hit .312, fifth best in the league behind Roberto Clemente's leading .329, Hank Aaron's .318, Willie Mays' .317, and Billy Williams' .315. No apologies are necessary for him not winning the batting title when you consider he was beaten out by four future Hall of Famers. He had 670 official times at bat; a league leading 209 hits, five more than teammate Vada Pinson's 204; 35 doubles; 11 triples; 69 walks; 117 runs scored, good for third place behind Tommy Helms' 126 and Willie Mays' 118; and a surprising 11 homeruns. And he played in all 162 games.

He also led the league in one unofficial category: most balls thrown back into the stands. It's always been Pete's belief that a ball hit into the stands should stay in the stands. "This is the only game I know where a guy will pay a hundred bucks for a seat in the hopes he'll get his hands on a three-dollar baseball." In other words, a ball hit into the stands belongs to the fans even if a fan dropped it back on the field or if it just landed in an empty section of seats and bounced back.

The Reds were a powerhouse of a team in 1965, but they just couldn't keep up with the Dodgers who won the pennant then defeated the Minnesota Twins in the World Series. Cincinnati finished fourth, and Dick Sisler was out of a job.

Pete was still growing up as a person and as a ballplayer when the 1966 season got under way. He was now a veteran of three full seasons and a recognized star of the game, but superstar status was still a few seasons away.

For the second straight year Pete hit over .300, going .313 in 156 games. He played third base for the first time in his career, being stationed on the hot corner for 16 games. He also had another 200-plus hits season, reaching safely 205 times in 654 trips up with 38 doubles, 5 triples, 16 homers, and 70 runs batted in.

The only statistic of Pete's that was off in 1966 was his number of runs scored: 97. But that's easily explained. This was the first year Frank Robinson played in an Oriole uniform because at age 32 the Cincinnati front office thought he was over the hill. He was so far over the hill that he won the Triple Crown in the American League. Pete lamented Robinson's departure because without the big outfielder with the big bat the Reds were rather punchless, and it showed in the National League's final standings.

Don Heffner took over as manager of the Reds at the start of the year but was replaced by Dave Bristol at mid-season. The Reds were 37-46 under Heffner and 38-37 under Bristol. The Dodgers repeated as NL Champs, only to get blown away in four straight in the World Series by Hank Bauer's Baltimore Orioles who had some of the best wings in baseball and proved it by shutting down Walter Alston's weak-hitting LA Bums for the last 34-plus innings of the series. The Reds finished a dismal seventh, ahead of expansion teams Houston and New York, the Mets' first season out of the cellar, and the hapless Chicago Cubs, managed by Leo "The Lip" Durocher who had said when he was hired after the Cubs had finished ninth in 1965, "This is not an eighth place club," and proved himself a prophet by finishing dead last.

The Cubs had gone 21 years without a pennant, one year more than the Reds had gone between 1940 and 1961. But the Cubs also had 20 consecutive seasons in the second division. At season's end, Pete and the Reds were wondering if the Reds were going the same way.

10

The Mail Bag

Every mailbag contains hundreds of requests for items to be used at auctions for one charity or another. These are worthwhile requests, but there just aren't enough items to send.

As the list of charities requesting donations from Pete grew, Pete had to discontinue giving to these mail-order charities. Instead he concentrated on charities located in Cincinnati.

There are always many requests for money ranging from $5 to hundreds of thousands of dollars. Pete makes a good salary and, like you and I, has to pay taxes and maintain his household. Just the postage expenses to mail autographed pictures gets to be rather large, not counting the cost of the photos.

People requested a car or when Pete gave the Reds coaches a jeep, there where hundreds of letters wanting Pete to donate them one too. There were many requests for free tickets. Some wanted one or two; others wanted 6-8 box seats.

Some fans sent baseballs for him to sign. We had to unwrap them, give them to Pete to sign, then rewrap and address the box. We've kept the local Post Office very busy over the years.

Pete's stamp bill is always staggering. We purchase rolls of stamps every day. When he was on his hitting streak, tens of thousands of letters arrived in a matter of weeks. Pete spent hours signing autographs for the fans.

Many letters contain self-addressed stamped envelopes. What a help they are! If more fans would do that, they would get their letters answered quicker.

A lot of the letters are cute and interesting. Most of the letters in this chapter speak for themselves.

Mr. Rose,

I've been sick this week, but seeing that yo signed your contract cheered me more than anything. My family are big Red fans and this is a vote of confidence for the year to come. My father loves your tactics and my mom wants to adopt yo and have you marry my sister. I think your a all around wonderful person and athlete. I know in my heart the Reds will take the Pennant and the series. Thanks for your time.

True Reds Fans,
Laura and family

Funny, isn't it? Moms want to adopt him; young girls want to marry him; young boys want to copy his style of playing and his hustle; and fathers are thankful that their children hold him up as their hero.

Dear Mr. Rose,

I am writing to you on behalf of my daughter. She doesn't know about this letter but I felt that I must try and contact you.

Several weeks ago she wrote you a lette that she spent days working on. She calls home from school every day hoping to hear from you.

My daughter's name is Juliann and in her letter she told you about her softball team and how she was chosen best third baseman in the league, and also picked for the All Star Game. She's a very good hitter and practised sliding from watching you. Also she has never played a game without a picture of Pete Rose in her back pocket for luck.

This will give you some idea of what you mean to this little girl. She even invited you for a big spaghetti dinner in our home if you are ever in our area.

I believe in her letter she asked if you could write to her or send her a special picture of yourself.

I am sure her letter either got lost or you haven't had time to read it yet.

Right now we are trying to make arrangements to get her to New York if it should turn out that the Yankees will make it to the World Series. To be able to see you in person would be a thrill she would never forget.

I know how busy you are but perhaps after the series you will have time to write her a brief ote or something. I just can't tell you how happy this little girl would be.

Sincerely
Mrs. Betty

Many, **many** mothers and fathers write to Pete about

their children, explaining how he is loved, copied and the children's all-around hero. This is just one more loving mother. Thanks for writing to Pete!

Dear Mr. Rose,

I have a 7 year old nephew who thinks you are the greatest thing going. He emulates your every move even up to the point of sliding head first all the time because he's seen you do it twice.

We all think it's great that such a great team player and clean cut person was chosen by him to copy and know nothing would thrill him more than a picture.

From the recent commercial you did, you're obviously not happy with the nickname "pink", but David is (my nephew). All his friends call him "pink rose" all the time — he's a hard charger and never quits — mostly due to you.

Sincerely,
   Thom

This lad is learning switch hitting and at a very young age. Good for him! Good luck to David and I hope the picture pleases him.

Dear Pete:

Congratulations on a great World Series championship. I can't write to all the players but I sure want to write to you.

In my opinion, this year as in so many other years, you are the key to the success of the Reds.

It really isn't important how much you hit a ball. Your fire, and love of the game radiates through the team and can be felt all over the ball park. I remember when Joe DiMaggio was hurt they used to say it made a difference to the team just to have him sitting on the bench. Thank God you're in good shape and a super player but I think you have the same effect on your team. I can't wait until next year starts.

Very truly yours,

Ed

I know of no one who loves the game as Pete does. He is very lucky that he has had no serious injuries. He really is a "spark plug" so to speak, of the team.

Dear Mr. Rose,

I realize that you must get tons of fan mail, and this letter is no exception, although I feel that it is a special one.

My mother, Wanda, is an avid Reds fan, and an even more avid fan of yours. She won't miss a game that the team plays, even if it means that the rest of the family don't get supper till the game is over. Whe the Reds win, we are treated to a great dinner, and a good mood on her part for days; if the Reds lose, it's MacDonald's for us, and she's not approachable for hours!

For Christmas this year, and to insure our meals being served on time, I'd like to give her something really special. Could you please autograph a photo of yourself to her; we'll hang it in the kitchen till baseball comes around again. She'd be thrilled, you can be assured, and the photo will be one of the best presents she'll ever receive.

Good luck to you and your team, and thanks for being one of the most colourful players in baseball!

Sincere Thanks From All of Us!

p. s. Please address the envelope to me at the above address to make sure she gets it as a Christmas surprise!

I say thank goodness for McDonald's once in awhile! But imagine a six or seven game losing streak by the Reds, hamburgers every night. My reaction is no thank you.

So here's hoping the picture made mother happy and a look at her favorite "star" will butter her up when the Reds lose and dinner will be served.

Dear Pete Rose,

How are you, will you send me a piece of your hair? A poster and you blood. A picture of your dog if you have one. Write me back a letter. Please. Thank you.

From,
Jamie

Dear Pete,

I'm writing to you about the comment the lady made about you and the underwear advertisement. I think you have a terrific body so why not show it off!

Good Luck,
Wendy

Dear Mr. Rose,

Please, Please, Please, Please, Please, Please, oh, Please!!! send me an autographed picture of yourself.   Thanks alot!

Ricardo

Dear Pete,

My friend and I were wondering a few things about you.

1. Do you go out on your wife?

2. Do you intend to?

3. Whats your address?

4. Do you ever plan to be in the general vicinity of RR 3 N. Manchester, Indiana, soon?

Also, do you plan to have any severe marital disasters in the near future?

I realize I am a very demanding person. If these criteria cannot be reached I guess I'll settle for an autographed picture of you. Oh by the way, you have the best body in baseball. Your face is second only to Steve Yeager's. I am not crazy, only a little mentally unbalanced.

Thank You,

Linda

The only comment I'll make is to say an autographed picture was sent to Linda.

Hi,

This is my third time to write you. If I could meet anybody in the whole world it would be you. I'm 16 now and ever since I was 5 I've loved you. When I was 6 for my birthday I got a Cincinatti Reds uniform even though I'm a girl. Your restaurant is my favorite. You have the best roast beef sand- wiches. I always get Pete's favorite when I go there. I have shole scrapbook on you.

Julie said she's been over to your house before. I could of died, cause I'd give anything to just meet you. Well I won't write too much cause I know you get alot of fan mail. If you get a chance I'd really appreciate it if you'd write back or send a picture to me.

Thanks for your time!
Love Ya,
  Viki
P.S. Some people think I look like you, and think I'm one of your kids!

I have a scrapbook of Pete too. Isn't is fun to look back at earlier years and read the articles that bring back so many memories? I know you are a beautiful young lady if you look like Pete. He is one handsome man when he is "all dressed up." Maybe one of these days your ultimate dream will come true and you will meet Pete. I truly hope so.

Dear Mr. Rose,
  This is the first time in my life I've written a letter of this nature, so it may be clumsy and stiff!
  We have a friendly battle going on in the convent over whom we like best, you or Johnny Bench. Of course, I'm for you. Her feastday (we celebrate our patron saint's day, instead of our birthday) is coming soon. And my request is this — would you please send this "Peacemaker" an autographed picture of yourself?
  Sister's name and address is: Sister Mary
  No doubt you understand, your fulfilling this request will give me more ammunition!
  God bless you and your family.
  Grateful,
    Sister Lucy

Nuns have fun too. I wounder if the picture really

gave her "points." Personally, I like Pete, but of course, I'm partial.

Dear Pete Rose,

I haven't heard from you lately. I hope everything is ok. My mother said she saw you recently on the Mike Douglas show. She said you gave them Pete Rose t-shirts. I was wondering how I could get one. Seeing as how I'm your number 1 fan, I really need one of your t-shirts. Please hurry and let me know how to get one, I'm glad baseball season is almost here. I really wish I lived near a stadium where the Reds played. Maybe I'll get a chance to go to a game soon. My sister said the Reds were going to on Superstars. I sure hope you win. I think Your the best. Good luck this season. I hope its the best ever!

   Love,
   Your number 1 fan,
   Kathy
P.S. Please rush me information on how to a t-shirt. I really truely want one.

There are tee-shirt speciality shops that imprint almost anything on tee-shirts. Also, we found some at a department store, so they are around.

Dear Pete,

I'm a fan of yours. I talked to you last summer at the Covington Kentucky Holiday Inn. I have Baseball card of you in 77, 76, 75, 74, 73, 72, in action, 70, 69, 68. That morning in Covington I was out by the swimming pool when I happened to look out in the parking lot, and my eyes literally popped out of my head! I ran over and jumped over the fence and said hi Pete!

There was only one thing wrong. I didn't have a pen and paper.
So now I'm asking you, could I have your autograph?
  Mike

Isn't it a surprise when you come upon a celebrity like Pete?

One morning before going to the stadium we stopped at a Big Boy Restaurant for breakfast. As we followed the hostess toward our seat, someone poked me and said, "Hi! How are you?" Guess who? Pete and Petey. It was a great surprise, and we did get to chat for awhile.

When people began recognizing him, they started asking for autographs and his breakfast sat getting cold. This is so very rude. Why can't they wait until after he has finished eating?

All public figures would be more willing to give autographs if some consideration would be given to them. There is a time and a place for seeking autographs.

Dear Pete,
  Though it may sound like a typical fan letter to you I want to tell you, you are the greatest! I am a seventeen year old girl and owe many thanks to you. It may sound strange but if you have time I will explain.
  Last year my school started a softball team no one really ever played before, but I had an edge, I use to play with my brother. Well the coach had me in left field and thought I could handle third. I was scared! The field was the field but third was something new, the hot corner! Well that weekend I went home and was my first Cincinnati game and, of course you. Gee was I

122   **Dear Pete**

happy when I saw the guy who did the belly slide also played third! From that day on I observed everything you did and tried to think the way you would. It must of worked because I won Two games by Pete Rose belly-slides (a little tougher for a girl, I'll asure you!) and this year I'm captain and have a shot at MVP!

I believe, also, that I owe my getting into college to you because captain of a Varsity sport does sound good when you plan to become a Physical Education teacher.

Well thanks again and you can be sure that when you play the Mets (or Yankees for that matter you will always have one person at Shea on your side even though it does cost my life

I was woundering why you crouch so on your batting stance would it help in Softball. Also do you have many girl fans?

If you are able to write back I would greatly appreciate it, but if not I will understand

Keep it up!! Your the best ever!!

With Love,

  Pam

Pete's batting stance is something else! I keep asking Tony where will the pitcher throw the ball in a couple of years? At the rate Pete's going, his strike zone will be zero.

I am glad your softball playing helped get you into college. Good luck to you.

Dear Mr. Rose,

A few weeks ago you marked autograph picture for my grandson Curt. I have another favor would you be kind enough to send another signed picture to "Bart" who is a sincere fan of

yours. When the autographed picture was given to my grand-
son Barts nose was surely out of joint at the time we requested
the the picture we never gone it a thought to ask for two. Would
you have a larger glossy photo if not the smaller one would suit
us fine.

May you have a very happy winter. Looking forward to
seeing you in the spring.

Sincerely yours,
  Lorranie B.

I hope Bart was pleased with his picture, even though
he had to wait a little for it. Grandchildren are precious.

Dear Mr. Rose,

Thank you so much for that photo. I don't recall asking for it,
I really appreciate it. I would have much rather have had a
letter but this is fine.

You have a lovely signature. Thanks a bundle for the auto-
graph!!

I'm so proud of it I took it to school and my English teacher
referred to me as a celebrity.

I'm really proud to have your autographed photo.

Thanks again.

Love,
  Becky

Pete just does not have the time to write letters. He
wishes he could answer each question, but the autographed picture will have to suffice for the fans at this
time.

Pete,

I didn't mention it in the letter that I wrote to you last week but I would be willing to pay you $5.00 a lesson if you would teach me to play baseball.

Sincerely
Jim

Dear Mr. Rose,

My name is Scot ——— I'm in the second grade, my babysitter is writing this for me. If possible, could you send me and my babysitter a picture of you with everybodys name on them. Please hurry and send them if you can because I'm driving Lisa my babysitter up the wall.

Lisa

Dear Mr. Rose,

I know you must get a lot of mail and a lot of requests for autographed pictures. However, this time I am sending you an autographed picture!

Now that you have my picture, I would love to have yours, Bigger, of course!

Best Regards,
Chad

Dear Mr. Pete Rose,

I am 11 years old and I am a big fan of yours. I would like to know if you would accept an invitation for dinner at my house. Any time will be convenient.

Sincerely,
Gary
P.S. I am looking forward to you coming if you accept.

Dear Mr. Rose,

I do head-first-slides just like you in Babe Ruth. I think they are fun but my coach doesn't like it. I got benched for six games once because he told me not to and he mentioned for me to steal third and I slid head first.

I think you're great and I would please like an autographed picture of you and the team.

Thanks,

Jeff

Dear Pete,

I understand that you bought Jeeps for your coaching staff. Although I am not on your coaching staff, I am sorely in need of a jeep.

I own a "69" VW. This morning I had a harrowing experience in that my windshield froze over and I almost had a grand slam in to a wall on my way to work. Therefore; you can see I'm in dire need of a jeep to get me thru the long, long cold New England winters.

You probably don't care, but if you should send me a jeep, I would like a red Jeep Renagade. Automatic if possible. You can have my VW as a conversation piece to put in your back yard, but please hurry as it is being surrounded by police and tow trucks.

Thanks

Dear Pete,

I have a poster of you on my closet door. When I get big I want to be a baseball player. Is it fun being a baseball player? I want to play first base or the outfield. How can you hit so good? Do you remember when you got in a fight with Bud Harrelson?

You killed him. Did you ever get in a fight with anyone else?
  Sincerely yours,
   Bobby

Pete did not *kill* Bud Harrelson! According to Pete it's fun being a basbeall player. He loves it! It takes a lot of work and dedication to succeed, but in all walks of life one has to apply oneself if they want to be a success.

Dear Mr. Rose,
  My younger brother, Dennis, has been playing pranks on the other kids in the neighborhood, telling them that you are our uncle. Would you please send him an autographed picture of yourself and sign it "from Uncle Pete." I know that he would really appreciate it.
  Sincerely yours,
   Beverly

I sent a picture to Dennis, but not signed by "Uncle Pete." Pete would not agree to such a thing, even for a joke.

Dear Mr. Rose:
  No offence but looking at your hair I keep wondering where on earth did you get that ridiculous hair comb.
  You look like a man, act like a man, but goodness will you please comb your hair like a man!
  A Frustrated Fan

Dear Pete,
  I am writing on behalf of my son Patrick, age 9.

Would it be possible to send him an autographed photo of you, his idol?

Patrick had been through a lot since December. He had a tumor on his head which left a hole in the skull the size of a silver dollar. It was removed in December and craniplastic surgury was in March to fill in the hole and cover it. We did a lot of traveling from home to childrens hospitals for 6 months.

It was not malignant and everything is fine now. He was allowed to play T ball wearing a special protective cap. Baseball and Pete Rose are his 1st loves.

He was so brave through it all. I would appreciate very much if you could reward him through my wishes.

Thank you

  Mrs.

P.S. We never miss a televised Reds game.

I hope Patrick has completely recovered from his ordeal. I know he is a brave lad. Hope he liked the autographed picture of Pete.

Dear Pete R.,

Thanks for making me a good baseball player. Because I copied your position and battin stance too, I have become a great ball player in the kid's minor league.

  Sincerely

  Brett

Dear Pete,

I'm Brett's Sunday School teacher a Sunday we learned about thanking others, so I told the kids to write a thank you letter to anyone they wanted, and I thought you would get a

kick out of this one.
   Brett's teacher
   Becky

Dear Pete,
   I'd like to hae an autographed picture. You probably won't think that request too unusual since you get hundreds like it each week, but I need a special message inscribed on this picture.
   You see, several weeks ago, I paid a visit to my home for my brother's wedding. At the post-reception party, my cousin remarked that he couldn't stand you and hoped you never got another hit in your life time.
   I always delight in giving unusual Christmas gifts to my friends and relatives. The thought struck me that we might be able to make Jim eat a few of his words if I could get you to send me a picture with an inscription such as: "Jim, I think you're a turkey, too!" or "Here's to you, . . ." — whatever, think up something more appropriate if yo so desire.
   Thanks much.
   Bill

Pete said, "No way."

Dear Pete,
   I'm writing for my son Tim, age 22, who is retarded. He has been a fan of yours and the whole Reds team for a long time. To him the Reds are the best win or lose. In fact, he's sad when you don't win. He wears his Cincinnati Championship shirt so ojᵣen, it's worn thin. The shirt was given to him from my daughter and son-in-law, who lived in Cincinnati and loved it

there.

Our whole family are avid fans of the Red's. We go into Philadelphia to see the games when you come into town. You can guess what shirt my son wears to the game.

Tim wants to know how he can get a Cincinnati Reds jacket. He's a big boy, about 170 lbs. and needs a large size. I would appriciate a reply.

Tim wanted to print a letter to you, but I don't think you could have read it, as he puts all the letters together. He understands most everthing that is said to him, but can't talk too much. Please understand, he sincerely loves the Cincinnati Reds. I told him I was writing to you, so I'm sure he'll be patiently waiting for you to answer.

Sincerely,

Mrs. Eleanore (Tim's mother)

An autographed picture was sent, and Tim's mother was advised that the stadium concessionaires and department stores in Cincinnati carry these jackets.

Dear Pete:

I have been addicted to you since I first saw you play when you were "rookie of the year". Your play then, as now, was exciting and breath-taking. I love to look at my old 1964 Red's Yearbook, and the pictures of you as a younger man. (I have a son, born the same year as you, 1941 — who lives and works in Saudi Arabia; if only he had been sports-minded!)

So thank you for making us kids again, as we are priveleged to see the games on TV, listen on radio, or see the games live at Riverfront. On the occasions when I get to see a game in Cincinnati, it seems that a sort of electricity runs through the

crowd when you step up to the plate. No fooling around with
hot dogs, beer, or popcorn, when Pete Rose is at bat!!

To millions of Americans, who love you, your playing makes
us forget for a while, the grimmer and seamier side of life as told
in the newspapers and seen on TV and heard on radio.

My dear, may you keep on thrilling us for many years; and
the very best of luck to the most vibrant personality of our
times.

Yours truly,
Eugenia M.

This great lady has said it all. Pete's fans really feel
this way, they forget their troubles, if just for awhile,
when they hear his plays on radio or see him in person
on T.V.

Dear Mr. Rose,
How can I thank you for calling Stevie? I'll start by telling
you how thrilled and honored he was. You are his idol and he
viewed that call as a dream come true. He wanted so badly to
ask you to come and see him that I felt compelled to convey his
message even though I know it is impossible for you at this
season. As with any child, he believes you can have anything if
you wish hard enough.

Stevie's parents are so grateful to you for taking time from
your busy schedule to make Stevie so happy. They are faced
with an awful certainty that Stevie will never leave the hospital. His doctor has removed the IVs and medication and
Stevie's real fight has begun.

I want you to know that I am so impressed with the com-
passion you have shown this dying boy. I will follow your

career with interest and best wishes. On behalf of Stevie, his parents, Alma, and myself I thank you again. You are a great guy.

 Sincerely,
  Brenda C. and Alma M.

P.S. Enclosed you will find a picture of Stevie. Alma supplied it since she though you'd like to see a guy who admires you so much.

Dear Mr. Rose:

 I am a 16 year old boy who lives in Atlanta, Georgia. I am going to be a professional baseball player. This is my only goal in life, exept for trying to be a good Christian. There is no doubt in my mind you are the greatest baseball player ever but, I want to say one thing and that is this "I am going to be better." I don't mean this to sound concided or snobish. I just think a guy has to have a certain amount of confidence in himself if he wished to sucide. I have this confidence in myself and know what I want to do. I would be very grateful if you would write me and give me a couple of pointers on how to make it to the Big Leagues. Thank you for your time and take it easy on the Braves this year.

 Sincerely,
  Tommy

No one will be rooting harder for Tommy than Pete.

Pete,

 Thank-you for sending Bobby, the card and he framed it and hung it on the wall. It is something he will never forget.

 There is no cure for this disease but with God, and people

like you, pills, lots of love and care. he might be able to live a normal life.

He is home now and doing just fine.

This is what he wanted me to give to you. A picture and letter from him to you with all the love in the world. Also he said, "Don't worry, you can the team will be World Champs this year.

Thanks'
   Uncle George and Bobby

I am a boy in Sweden how play baseball. A friend to had the address to you and said that I could write. And now I have dane that.

I like you and Jonny Bench very much. And i will ask you if send me a poster on you and if will write your name on it and if you can send me 1-3 the "Reds" decal. I scoud be very glad. How man matches have you play on this sesong?
   Per Holm
My Englis is not so god but I hope you show could read this letter.

This letter is from a fan in Sweden. I don't know if they play baseball in Sweden, most young children overseas play soccer.

Mr. Rose,

I am in the U.S. Army an currently stationed over here in Europe, which is not exactly exciting, but as a professional soldier this is my job and duty in which I am representing my country.

I wanted to take this time to write a tremendous ballplayer

Dear Pete   **133**

representing our country also. I feel you are the greatest all-around ballplayer that ever lived. I think the day that you say good-bye to baseball, will be a day in which baseball should be in sorrow. You have been my favorite player since I was young enough to know about the great game of baseball. I wish you and the Reds nothing but the best of luck always. It would make me very happy if you could send me a personally autographed picture of yourself. Thank you very much for your time.

Sincerely,
Allen R.

11

Stardom

Pete was still living in a dream world when the 1966 season ended. Before the next campaign began, he woke up.

During the off-season, Pete got to meet his boyhood hero but not in the usual way or under normal circumstances.

Toward the end of the 1966 season, Pete was approached with the idea of visiting the American servicemen in Vietnam to help build their morale, as the saying goes. He was cool to the idea until he was told that Joe DiMaggio would be going along. That's all Pete had to hear. If it meant meeting "Joltin' Joe", he'd walk into the mouth of Hell.

DiMaggio had been Pete's idol when Pete was playing Knot Hole baseball in Cincinnati. He knew everything about Joe, being able to recite his statistics from a keen memory for such facts. DiMaggio had won the American League batting title in 1939 (.381) and in 1940 (.352). In 1939 and in 1941 he was voted the

Dear Pete   **135**

American League's Most Valuable Player.

Pete met DiMaggio at DiMaggio's restaurant in San Francisco, down on Fisherman's Wharf. They later boarded a jet at Travis Air Force Base north of the city and flew to Vietnam by way of Anchorage, Alaska and Japan. After 17 hours in the plane with only a refueling stop in Tokyo, they landed in Saigon.

After arriving in Vietnam, Pete met actress-singer Martha Raye who was an old friend of DiMaggio. Ms. Raye was there as part of a USO-type show, the kind Bob Hope is always doing. Also in Pete's group was Bob Fishel, the public relations director for the Yankees.

Pete wrote a whole chapter about his Vietnam experience in his 1970 autobiography. It was due more to the fact that the war over there was still going on in 1970 than anything else. He still recalls very vividly many of the sights he saw: so many young men with limbs blown off, with disfigured faces, little Vietnamese children half-starved, bombed out buildings and villages, etc.

Pete's trip to Vietnam helped to mature Pete as a person. Until that first day in Saigon, Pete had lived a sort of dream life. He had grown up in a Tom Sawyer/ Huckleberry Finn sort of way, and after reaching adulthood, he was allowed to continue that life by playing baseball for money. Vietnam awakened him to the real world where people fight and die so others can live and be peaceful, where life isn't nine innings today and another game tomorrow.

With the Vietnam tour behind him but with the memory of it etched deeply in his mind, Pete turned his attention to the new baseball season of 1967.

Dave Bristol and his wad of tobacco were still at the Reds' helm. Cincinnati fared better the second time around under Bristol, but they were only good enough for a fourth place finish inspite of being 12 games over .500. The St. Louis Cardinals, after a mid-season rush by the surprising Chicago Cubs, took the pennant with Bob Gibson's pitching and Lou Brock's hitting and base-stealing. Gibson then beat the Boston Red Sox and Carl Yastrzemski in the World Series in seven games.

Pete had some decent numbers, hitting .301 in 158 games, 123 games in the outfield and 35 at second base. His number of times at bat declined to 585 as did his number of hits, 176, of which 32 were doubles, 8 triples, and 12 homeruns. And he only scored 86 runs in 1967, drew 56 walks, and fanned 66 times. Then just like that the season was over.

The following year of 1968 Pete faced a new challenge: the dreaded DL, disabled list. He broke his thumb and missed three weeks of play. That's when he learned he's only a good fan when he's playing the game, not just watching it.

Inspite of the the injury, Pete won his first National League batting title with a .335 mark; 626 times at bat, 210 hits, 42 doubles, 6 triples, and 10 homeruns.

Although Pete and some of his teammates had an outstanding year, the Reds under Bristol for the third year remained locked in fourth place, 14 games behind front-runner St. Louis. The Cardinals made it look easy again, although they did have to stave off another mid-season push by Chicago. But unlike 1967, the Redbirds didn't win the World Series. They faced the Detroit Tigers who had made a mockery of the American League pennant race behind the pitching of 31-game winner Denny McLain and lefty Mickey Lolich. Until the fifth inning of the seventh game, it appeared the Cardinals would repeat as World Champions. Then Lou Brock was thrown out trying to steal second, a fact that must have bothered him because in the following Detroit at-bat he misplayed a line drive off the bat of Mickey Stanley that turned the tide in Detroit's favor. Lolich won his third game of the series, and the Tigers brought the trophy back to the Motor City.

"Wait till next year," the Reds kept saying in the clubhouse when the season ended.

Expansion hit the Big Leagues again in 1969. The American League added teams in Seattle and Kansas City, the Royals replacing the A's who had been moved to Oakland by owner Charles Finley. The National League brought an international flavor to the Majors by granting a franchise to a group in Montreal. San Diego also got a team.

Looking over Pete's career statistics, it could be said that 1969 was the year he peaked as a player. Of course, this isn't true, although he did have his best year for homeruns with 16, RBIs 82, triples 11, and batting average .348, which was good enough to win him a second straight hitting title. But Pete also hit 16 round-trippers in 1966 and had 11 triples in both 1965 and 1972. The .348 BA and 82 RBIs held up, but in all other categories he had his best years ahead of him.

Pete made the National League All-Star team for the

fourth time in his young career. He had been selected as one of the league's best in 1965, 1967, and 1968, but he didn't play in '68 because of an injury. Through '69, he had yet to get his first All-Star game hit.

With expansion, the Major Leagues divided into divisions, each league splitting up somewhat geographically. The American League did it straight east and west: New York, Boston, Baltimore, Cleveland, Detroit, and Washington in the East; and Chicago, Minnesota, Kansas City, California, Oakland, and Seattle in the West. The National League had to be different, putting Cincinnati and Atlanta in the West with Los Angeles, San Francisco, San Diego, and Houston. Logically, it would seem that Chicago and St. Louis, who were placed with Pittsburgh, Philadelphia, New York, and Montreal in the East, should have been in the West instead of the Reds and the Braves. But whoever said the Powers-that-be in Major League Baseball had any logic?

The new set-up presented some very interesting pennant races. The schedules were arranged in such a way that each team played each team in their own division home-and-away one time around, then played the teams in the other division home-and-away one time around. They did this twice during the course of the year, then finished the season by playing strictly within their own divisions in order to determine divisional champions for the play-offs in October.

Odds-makers had the Chicago Cubs as the best bet to win the National League East. Leo Durocher had put together a solid club that had plenty of power, good pitching, and sound defense. They were missing only two key elements: a regular centerfielder and a good bench. On April 1, the Cubs were 8-5 favorites.

In the West, the smart money was split between the San Francisco Giants and the Reds. The Dodgers were fading fast in Los Angeles with the retirement of "Dandy" Sandy Koufax and the aging of stars like Don Drysdale and Maury Wills. Houston was still trying to put a full-fledged major league team on the field, and the Braves were short on pitching. For Cincinnati, it looked like "next year" had finally arrived.

The Cubs started the season on a roll and kept rolling right into August, building a lead of 9½ games over the surprising New York Mets. Then the roof caved in on Chicago as that lack of a bench finally took its toll. The Mets, although not having the quality players the Cubs had, suddenly became world-beaters on the strength of a strong pitching staff that included future Hall-of-Famers Tom Seaver, Jerry Koosman, and Nolan Ryan and standout reliever Tug McGraw. New York overtook the Cubs and won the division going away.

The West was another story completely. Just about every team except San Diego took a turn at leading the division. Finally, it came down to the Giants, Reds, and Braves.

Going into the last week of the season, the division title was still up for grabs. The Reds could determine their own destiny, and that suited them just fine. They went into Los Angeles with a chance to put themselves into first for good, but a season full of sore arms caught up with them. Mel Queen, Gerry Arrigo, Jim Maloney, and Gary Nolan had suffered from one ailment or another during the year, and they were needed badly if the Reds were to win the division. They dropped a doubleheader to the Dodgers, then moved on to Houston where a rookie named Keith Lampart hit a ninth inning homer off Wayne Granger that eliminated Cincinnati from contention. The Reds finished third, four games behind Atlanta and San Francisco.

The year 1969 was not without its exceptional highlights. On April 30, Jim Maloney pitched a no-hitter over the Houston Astros in Cincinnati, and the next day Houston's Don Wilson returned the favor by no-hitting the Reds. It was only the second time in history that back-to-back no-hitters had been thrown.

About the most memorable moment for Pete, other than his batting title, came in the outfield. Pete was playing center and Alex Johnson was in left; Johnson was there because leftfield is the easiest position to field and the Reds needed his bat in the lineup. The Reds were playing in Atlanta, and a Braves' hitter smacked one to left that looked like a sure-fire homer. Johnson ran back to the fence, and Pete raced over from center. Johnson leaped high and slapped at the ball, just trying to keep it in play. The ball popped into the air and came down in Pete's glove for a 7-8 putout. Later that year Johnson dropped a routine liner, and his response to Pete was, "Where were you?"

The season ended and so did Dave Bristol's tenure as manager of the Reds. General manager Bob Howsam fired Bristol, and on October 9 he hired 36-year-old Sparky Anderson to guide the club the following year.

Anderson had played second base in the minors but not too well. He turned to managing early on, holding the reins at Rock Hill in the Western Carolina League, St. Petersburg in the Florida State League, Modesto in the California League, Asheville in the Southern League, and Toronto in the International League before joining the San Diego Padres as a coach in 1969. When he joined the Reds, he was walking into a situation similar to the one Earl Weaver had entered in Baltimore. He had a team with all the right parts except an ignition switch. Weaver turned on the Orioles, and Anderson was ready to take the club Howsam had assembled and turn it on.

During Bristol's term as manager, Howsam had replaced most of the stars from the 1961 pennant-winning team. Pete had been an interim addition, coming onto the Reds between 1961 and Bristol's first year. Veteran Don Blasingame was the first of the 1961 squad to go. Tony Perez became a regular in 1965 at first base but was moved to third in 1967 when Howsam brought in Lee May to play first. Tommy Helms, who had played third the year before and had won Rookie-of-the-Year honors, was moved to second. Catcher Johnny Bench became the Reds' third Rookie-of-the-Year in 1968. Shortstop Woody Woodward and pitchers Clay Carroll and Tony Cloninger came over from Atlanta in a June trade that same year. In the off-season Vada Pinson was sent to the Cardinals for outfielder Bobby Tolan and pitcher Wayne Granger. Pitcher Jim Merritt was acquired from Minnesota, also that winter.

On paper Cincinnati appeared to be missing only one

more solid outfielder and some sound pitching arms.

As the cold winds of the north blew into the Ohio Valley, Anderson went to Florida to look at some minor league prospects, hoping to find those missing elements.

Of course, Pete was eager for the new season to begin, but he could look back over the previous three seasons with pride in his accomplishments. He had made the All-Star team each of those years, and he had hit over .300, winning batting titles in 1968 and 1969, neither one having come easy.

In 1968, he was a point ahead of Matty Alou as the season entered its final weekend. Pete went 5-for-5 on the next to last day against the Giants, but Alou was 4-for-4 against the Cubs. Alou actually gained a fraction of a point because he had fewer times at-bat. On the last day, Pete banged out a single against Ray Sadecki and went 1-for-3. All Alou had to do was go 2-for-5 or just 1-for-2 to win the title, but he went 0-for-4.

In 1969, Pete was being pressed by the great Roberto Clemente for the title. Going into the final day, Pete knew it would take a perfect game by Clemente and a nothing game by him for the Pirates' outfielder to win. Pete felt fairly confident that the championship was his until a fan yelled out to him that Clemente was 3-for-3 when Pete was coming up for his fourth plate appearance of the day, already having gone 0-for-3. The Reds were already out of the race, and the Braves, the team Cincinnati was playing, had already won the division. So the only thing left was for Pete to win the batting title. If anything more had been at stake, Pete would have swung away, but he didn't. Instead he put down a perfect bunt and beat it out for a hit. In the meantime, Clemente drew a walk and made an out in his final two trips up, and Pete won the championship for the second year in a row.

Pete also passed a few career milestones in the 60s. He got his 500th hit off Al Jackson of the New York Mets at Shea Stadium in New York on September 16, 1965, and his 1000th hit came off Dick Selma on June 26, 1968 at Crosley Field. He won his first Gold Glove Award in 1969. He ended the decade by hitting over .300 for the fifth consecutive year.

For a lot of baseball players, Pete Rose had already played a full career. But Pete was only 28 years old. He figured he had at least another dozen years left. Besides his own personal goals, he had three very important team goals left to achieve: a division championship, a National League pennant, and a World Series title. It was with those three aims in mind that he looked forward to playing in the 70s.

12

With a Little Bit of Help

Two of our daughters helped address envelopes and insert autographed pictures. The four of us worked 10 hours a day trying to get the mail answered. We received all kinds of letters; birth announcements, wedding invitations, graduation announcements, Bar Mitzvahs. All asked Pete to honor them with his presence at their joyous occasion. Parents would ask Pete to write a letter to their son or daughter. Some of the kids had trouble in school, were on drugs, or had trouble with the law. All hoped the letter would straighten out their child. They had faith in Pete.

The mail also included congratulatory letters from people from all walks of life, including congressmen, ministers, sports-writers, teachers, principals, etc. Some letters included invitations for speaking engagements. Some announced banquets. There were thousands of invitations. If he went to every one he was invited to, we would weigh in at 300 pounds come spring training.

With so much mail, sometimes it would take me two months to answer some letters. This was especially true on several occasions when we got three or four bags full, each containing thousands of letters. By the time we got to the letter, the event was over with. We apologize to all the fans, but there is only so much you can do in a day.

Dear Mr. Rose,

How proud your family must be of your great achievements, a fine gentleman, and a great athlete.

We as parents can truly understand what they feel. Our son is also in professional baseball and when he reaches his highest we hope he handles it in the same way you did, with honor, dignity and class.

Respectfully,
Robert and Nellie

This letter is from the parents of one of the Dodger players. Pete could ask for no higher praise than the thoughts of this great couple on his achievements.

Dear Mr. Rose,

I am the athlete director at the American High School in Spain. Living outside the U.S. as we do, I make every effort to keep our young athletes excited and informed about outstanding athletes in the U.S. There is certainly no doubt about the tremendous job that you are doing!

I would like to make a bulletin board in my office featuring your picture form S.I. for the kids to enjoy. Would you be so kind as to autograph it for me and return it in the enclosed

envelope.
Let me wish you continued good luck.
Sincerely yours,
Norm

This letter from Spain explains how popular Pete is world wide. His dedication is contagious, everyone wants to be a part of it.

Dear Pete Rose,
Congratulations to not only a great baseball player but a gentleman. I just watched you on the "Phil Donahue" show and thought any youngster watching the show would learn a lesson in loyalty and fair play.
There are fans in New York and New Jersey who are proud of you and I am one of them.
I'd greatly appreciate an autographed picture for my grandson Sean and only hope when he grows up he will have you an an ispiration.
Thank you and best of luck in the future to not only a marvelous baseball player but a decent man.
Sincerely,
Doris

Another grandmother who wants her son to use Pete as a guide to follow as he is growing up. Dedication to whatever you are doing will help achieve the goals one sets for oneself.

Pete,
As a life long fan of the Reds and an avid Pete Rose fan since

1963, I wanted you to know what the people of Virginia think about you. --- When one is mentioned in the same breath with Jefferson, Madison, and Monroe, around here, he has to be something. Wishing you the best year ever (World Series hero maybe?) and many more to come.
  Sincerely,
    Woody

Thank you, Woody. This really is high praise!

Dear Pete,
  The excitement you give to baseball is the greatest gift that you can give to mankind. We are always watching to see what you will do next to win for the Reds.
  You have lived Reds baseball along time and we as spectators are blessed because of it. We live where every one around us is a Philies fan yet we are always boosting the Reds. If you could see our house you would think we were part of the team. We have wastebaskets, pennants, balls autographed hanging on the lamp chains, all showing that the Reds are the greatest.
  I also have a husband who is the greatest, and his 40th birthday is coming up March 18th. I would like to give him a special gift, that is messages from the Reds team. I am asking you to send this post card back to me with a message on it so that I can give them to him on his birthday. Thank you for being who you are. My husbands name is Ed. Good luck in the coming season and I hope that another series will be yours.
  Sincerely,
    Suzannn

Pete takes a break from spring training in'76.

Pete comes home to Cincy for the first time as a Phillie.

The righthanded batting stance.

Pete has always been the main attraction for the media.

Taking his cuts as an Expo in spring training, 1984.

Pete signs autographs at Reds' training camp, 1985.

Backyard and pool at Pete's house.

One of the restaurants Pete owned at one time or another.

Pete and author Helen Fabbri in Pete's kitchen
after a long session with the mail, 1979.

Helen and Pete pose for a friend at a restaurant.

Author Helen Fabbri looks over some of Pete's
memorabilia she has collected over the years.

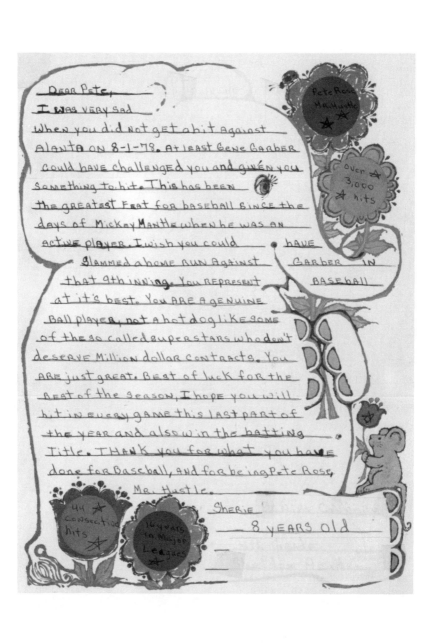

Dear Pete,
I was very sad when you did not get a hit against Alanta on 8-1-78. At least Gene Garber could have challenged you and given you something to hit. This has been the greatest feat for baseball since the days of Mickey Mantle when he was an active player. I wish you could have slammed a home run against that 9th inning. You represent at it's best. You are a genuine ball player, not a hot dog like some of the so called superstars who don't deserve Million dollar contracts. You are just great. Best of luck for the rest of the season, I hope you will hit in every game this last part of the year and also win in the batting Title. THANK you for what you have done for Baseball, and for being Pete Rose, Mr. Hustle.

have Garber in baseball

Pete Rose Mr. Hustle

over 3,000 hits

44 consecutive hits

16 years in Major Leagues

Sherie
8 years old

ROSE GETS HIT

3,◯◯◯

To Pete,
    Congragulations for your 3,000th hit. I hope you can get 4,000 hits when the season ends. Hope the Reds can get passed the Giants and go to the World Series. I've got 6 autograph pictures and 2 reguler autographs. Last year I played for a baseball team and my number was the same as yours! I still play for a team. Hope you and the Reds do good.
    Sincerely, Mark Neese

P.S.

A picture of me

Youth Forest in the
American Bicentennial National Park In Israel

פרק יובל האמאתים של ארצות הברית

JEWISH NATIONAL FUND

קרן קימת לישראל

In Honor Of

PETER EDWARD ROSE

Planted By

Todd

TREE

Dear Pete Rose,
    My name is Mary
I am 12 years old and a Reds
Fan and a Pete Rose Fan. It
seems to me that money is
more important to you than
the Reds. So if you will
remain on Cincinnati I will
send you my life time savings
of $492.32 wich Im saving
for College But to me you
on the Reds is more important

        Love Always
        Mary

PS If you go to another
  team dont make it
  the yankees.
    (I hate the yankees)

Stay Sweet
as sweet and
handsome as
you are.

PETE,
Hey what's Happining? Nothin
that Much around here. Well I
think you're a really "FOXY lookin,"
guy I wish you would send me
a picture of your Foxy self!!
I really think your a good
player. well I hope I'll be
Seeing Around!! Wow!!! Your
Fantastic!! I wish I could
meet you in Person, See ya.
Stay cool

                    Yours Truely,
  Send me a   Michete
picture,

  "Foxy Lookung"!.

THE CINCINNATI ENQUIRER

FINAL EDITION/NEWSSTAND PRICE 35¢   THURSDAY, SEPTEMBER 12, 1985   A GANNETT NEWSPAPER

4,192: Pete Singles Past Ty Cobb

Tim Sullivan

Numbers Don't Tell Full Story

Now that Pete Rose has the record we have anticipated so long, it should be remembered that he never needed it.

It is the milestone of his baseball career, not the measure. It is his landmark, not his legacy.

No, anyone who would appraise Pete Rose would be wrong to do so by the numbers. For he is not so much a ballplayer as he is an emotion, an attitude, a symbol. "Pete Rose," Commissioner Peter Ueberroth said, "is baseball."

He is, at least, what baseball ought to be. In our time, perhaps in all time, no one has played this boy's game so boyishly.

He perfected the head-first slide and has turned even the inning-ending putout at first base into a stylish celebration. The wonder of Pete Rose is that baseball has no drudgery for him. If he is a hot dog, it is because he plays the game with so much relish.

"He should bypass the Hall of Fame," Steve Garvey says, "and go straight to the Smithsonian."

HE IS, in short, an original. Four thousand, one hundred and ninety-two hits no better define Pete Rose than five acids define Hamlet. In both cases, the play's the thing.

Rose's pages in the record books, to borrow a line he once used for his paycheck, could be piled so high that a show dog couldn't jump over them. Yet future generations could not fully appreciate him without film: the All-Star collision with Ray Fosse, the playoff bout with Bud Harrelson, the autumn evening in 1975 when he turned to Carlton Fisk and said, "Ain't it great just to be playing a game like this."

Just as easily, though, the footage could come from lesser contests, for Pete Rose views every game with glee—the arctic nights in San Francisco, the Saharan afternoons in St. Louis, the two-night doubleheaders of long-lost pennant races.

"I live for baseball," he says.

THE RECORD he reached Wednesday is merely the measure of that devotion. It represents 23 seasons of fighting fatigue and ignoring aches, of wanting things a little more and a lot longer than the next guy.

It does not mean he is the greatest hitter of all-time. It does not even mean he is the greatest hitter of his own time. "It will mean," Rose says simply, "that I'm the guy with the most hits."

This does not diminish the accomplishment; rather it makes it all the more extraordinary. It is a triumph of desire over talent, of endurance over opportunity.

It is Cinderella landing the prince, Galahad locating the Grail. It is justice served and romance rewarded.

It is exactly what Pete Rose deserves.

Tim Sullivan is sports columnist for The Enquirer.

PETE ROSE hits an Eric Show pitch for a single to left-center field Wednesday night to become baseball's all-time hit leader.

The Cincinnati Enquirer/Annette Kraft

Memory Will Last Forever

BY HOWARD WILKINSON
The Cincinnati Enquirer

When Pete Rose hit the magic 4,192nd hit Wednesday, he made 47,237 memories that will last just as many lifetimes.

You could see it in the eyes of Tina McGary, sitting behind home plate in the blue seats and wishing she could run out to first base and kiss the 44-year-old ballplayer. It was the same player she watched play high school ball at Western Hills a quarter of a century ago.

It was in the eyes, too, of 11-year-old Brad McGinnis of Chillicothe. He strained to see over the heads of the grown-ups in front of him for the sight he'll be able to describe to his children's children some day when he's old and gray.

He'll tell of a cool September evening when a ballplayer named Rose stepped to the plate, took the count to 2-1, and lofted a ball into left center field that seemed to hang in the crisp air forever before coming down with a bounce on the Riverfront AstroTurf.

When it did, it let loose magic.

WAVE AFTER wave of cheers rocked the perfect circle of a stadium, from the box seats behind home plate to the highest reaches of the red.

Flashbulbs exploded; fireworks shot into the air; his teammates surged onto the field to congratulate the man who, in a short year, has brought them from nothing to something special, indeed.

"I don't think I'll ever feel this way again," said Esther Peterson of Dayton, standing behind the blue seats on the

left-field line, tears rolling down her cheeks.

"He's the fans' player. I feel like we're part of everything he does. And this is the greatest thing he's ever done."

After six minutes of bedlam, the cheers had just begun to subside when Rose's son, Petey, dressed as always in his No. 14 uniform, came onto the field and hugged his dad at first base.

The sight just set the crowd off again.

"HE IS what baseball is all about," said Greg Mantz of Trenton, watching from the green seats on the third base line. "He did it all on his own. He showed us what hard work and determination could bring."

7th-Inning Triple Adds No. 4,193

BY GREG HOARD
The Cincinnati Enquirer

Pete Rose tried but could never quite capture the words. He could never describe what it meant to him to pass Ty Cobb.

But Wednesday night he showed us. He stood at first base and cried.

At 8:01 p.m., Pete Rose slapped a 2-and-1 pitch from Eric Show into left-center field for the 4,192nd hit of his career.

Then the wave of affection took over. At first, Rose tried to hold back the tears. He tried to take all of it in stride: the cheers, the handshakes, the congratulations from his teammates and the San Diego Padres, the cheers from 47,237 fans that went on for seven minutes.

But this was too big, too much. It had taken too long, and it had taken more effort than anyone would ever realize.

Rose could not handle this alone. When he could no longer fight the tears, he turned to Tommy Helms, the Reds' first base coach and a friend for years. He clutched Helms around the neck and shoulders and sobbed.

"I don't know what to do," he told Helms.

Helms replied: "That's OK, Boss. You're Number One. You deserve it all."

"I WAS awful lonely standing out there at first base," Rose said later, during a ceremony after the Reds' 2-0 victory. "I can't describe what was going through my mind, what was going through my stomach ..."

"I wish everyone in baseball could go through what I went through tonight at first base. I was all right until I looked up in the air. I looked up in the air and I saw my dad and Ty Cobb. That took care of me."

With Rose sobbing, Helms turned and motioned toward the dugout. Rose's son, Petey, came to his father's side, and the scene was repeated.

This hit was one for the heart, as well as the record book.

It didn't take long. It happened just 11 minutes after the game began, on Rose's first trip to the plate.

Eddie Milner, the lead-off hitter, was out on an infield pop-up. Rose went to the batter's box with the same determined look he has worn since 1963, his rookie season.

Show's first pitch was a fastball, and Rose let it go for a ball. Rose fouled the next pitch back for a strike. Rose took the third pitch, a slider, for another ball.

With each pitch, the standing-room-only crowd stood taller, craning their necks for a better look. At 8:01, they saw.

THE HIT was like many others in Rose's career. It left the bat on a line, headed for the alley between left and center field. Carmelo Martinez gave chase from left field, and Kevin McReynolds from center, but to no avail. This was Rose's "Big Knock," the record breaker.

Fireworks exploded. Rose's teammates left the dugout en masse. Two of his oldest friends, Tony Perez and Davey Concepcion, hoisted him on their shoulders. Marge Schott, the Reds' president, was led to field. And a red Corvette, specifically designed for Rose and this moment, was driven onto the field. It's license plate said, "PR 4192."

After the game, President Reagan telephoned with congratulations. "In this Pete Rose, alias Charlie Hustle?" And Schott presented Rose with a silver punch bowl, a silver tray and 12 silver cups.

"I'm not smart enough," Rose said, "to come up with the words to show my appreciation for the fans."

Not long ago, Rose described his hit as something "that will affect me years from now, I'm talking about way down the road."

Here is a true Reds fan, everything from Redland. Hope the card was received in time for her husband's birthday.

Dear Pete,

I know it's been along time and you've probably heard from every member of your high school class — I thought I'd make sure you'd heard from everyone, and just drop you a line.

If you're wondering by now "who is he?" — just look in the Western Hills Yearbook the year you were in the 10th grade. I remember we had gym and English together. The kids form your neighborhood would get with the kids from mine and go at it after school and even on weekends. It's hard to believe that from that group a "Super Star" emerged. It's been so long ago though. I don't expect you to remember.

I've followed your career since you started with Cincinnati. Back when we were in school together the Reds had such stars as "Big Klu", Wally Post, Gus Bell, Johnny Temple, Roy McMillian, and there of course Frank Robinson was coming along. None of them, however, could match you in 'hustle', 'desire', and all out ability. Now at the end of a fantastic season (I'm so glad somebody 37 can show them we can still move). Even though the pennant escaped, it looks like the future for you will be even better. If the Reds would ever be stupid enough to allow you to leave, they'll have one less fan, too.

One of the reasons I'm writing is to tell you how you helped me with my students. Oh, yeah, I forgot to tell you about my career — just an'ole' school teacher down here in Jackson, Mississippi. Anyway, I just happened to catch the Phil Donahue show on which you appeared (we get it late here in Jackson, it was around Sept. 18th). You came over real well

Dear Pete   **149**

and I thought of an idea you could use to help me. Kids, today, are real gone on sports heroes, so when I mentioned, and just had my yearbook to back me up, that I went to school and knew Pete Rose, it made me an instant somebody. The reaction was great. I was surprised that not only the kids were impressed, but many of the other faculty members as well. After I had made it very clear that I had taught you everything you knew, the roar of laughter settled down. It was a nice day or two around here, though.

Another reason for writing to you is that among the really inpressed was my 10 yr. old son, Kevin, who has simply styled his life after yours -- eats and sleeps baseball. He, along with about 20 others, would really like an autographed picture -- I don't know if it's possible, but it would really make him happy.

Well, if you every get to Mississippi, give me a call and we'll roll out the "Red" carpet. Sure wish we had the funds to get you to speak at our Athletic Banquet in April, the kids would really love it. If you can, send a couple of pictures and just drop a line with them as to what your fee would be, maybe there would be a way. Again thanks alot for the many good times on T.V. and remember a lot, and I mean a lot, of kids really look up to you. It's got to be a nice feeling. Good luck with the Reds.

Your friend,
Terry,

An old school buddy of Pete's, who is impressed that one of the "gang" has made it to the top in his field. Likewise, Terry has accomplished much in his career as a teacher and must be a very dedicated individual!

13

Two Wins and a Loss

A year to remember, 1970. For Pete, it may be the
most memorable year of his life.

Spring training in Florida was unlike any other Pete
had known before. Cincinnati had a new manager in
George "Sparky" Anderson and some new players in
Pedro Borbon, Jim McGlothlin, and Dave Concepcion.
But most of all the Reds would have a new place to play
by mid-season.

Sparky Anderson made his first team move during
the winter. He named Pete to be captain of the Reds.
There had been no captains under Dave Bristol because Bristol felt he didn't need one. Anderson believed every good army — and what is a sports team if
not an army by a different name? — needs a leader in
the field as well as at headquarters. So he picked the
man who had been with the Reds the longest and who
had the respect and admiration of his teammates.

The first task of a new manager is to get to know his
players. Having been a coach with San Diego the year

before, Anderson was at least acquainted with Cincinnati's veterans, but he was unfamiliar with most of the minor leaguers. This was good because he had no preconceived ideas about the youngsters. So it was only natural that he would give them all long looks during the exhibition season.

The Reds had a basic problem that seems to be the malady that makes most teams into also-rans. Cincinnati lacked enough quality pitching to sustain a pennant drive. There were certainly a lot of experienced arms in camp, but too many of them were tired, exhausted from overuse in previous campaigns. Anderson saw this right away and started looking for fresh talent among the rookies.

And he found it in Wayne Simpson and Don Gullett, a couple of fireballers with limited professional playing time. Anderson subscribed to the theory that a good fastball can make up for inexperience.

By the time Opening Day arrived, the Reds had a set lineup and a potentially awesome starting rotation. Johnny Bench was secure behind the plate. Lee May provided power at first. Tommy Helms had second nailed down tight. Tony Perez manned the hot corner. The outfield had Pete in right, Bobby Tolan in center, and youthful Bernie Carbo in left, replacing Alex Johnson who had been traded to California. Shortstop was being shared by Woody Woodward and newcomer Concepcion. The five starters on the mound were Jim Merritt, Gary Nolan, McGlothlin, Gullett, and Simpson, and Wayne Granger and Clay Carroll provided some superb relief help from the bullpen.

On paper the Reds had it all: a good blend of high average hitters and power hitters, speed, defense, and pitching. But pennants aren't won on paper. So only one question remained.

It's said that a baseball season can be divided into thirds. No matter what, the law of averages say a Major League baseball team will win one-third of its games and it will lose one-third of its games. It's the other third that determines where a team finishes in the standings.

It's also said that a manager really does not have much to do with whether his team wins or loses in 90% of its games, that winning and losing is determined by the players on the field. But the manager does affect the other 10% of his team's games very directly. His decisions in those 16 or so games are the proof of his ability to manage.

So the question was: Could Sparky Anderson make the right decisions and direct his team to a title?

The answer was six months away.

Even further into the future another question would be answered. Boy or girl? With the beginning of the season, Pete's wife Karolyn gave him the wonderful news that she was expecting their second child. The baby was due in November. Good timing. Pete would have enough distractions as the campaign wore on.

Crosley Field had known many great moments over the years, and almost all the greats played there at least once, including many American Leaguers who faced the Reds in a World Series or two. The Reds could trace their history back to 1869 with the forming of the first all-professional team. They had known triumph and defeat and had been the unwitting benefactors of Major League Baseball's biggest embarrassment, the 1919 "Black Sox Scandal". They had won four pennants and two World Series in the "modern" era, but Cincinnati couldn't point to any past team and call it one of the all-time greats.

Well, nothing lasts forever, and the old must make way for the new.

Major League Baseball had become "Big Business" in the 1960s, thanks to television and a little help from the Supreme Court in the early 1950s when the justices saw fit to exempt Baseball from anti-trust laws. The owners were taking in more money than ever before, and they were paying out more, too, to players who demanded and got bigger and bigger contracts. With salaries escalating faster than revenues, something had to be done to increase cash flow.

The Boston Braves, Philadelphia Athletics, and St. Louis Browns came up with a unique idea on how to raise bigger bucks. The Braves moved to Milwaukee in 1953, and the Athletics headed west to Kansas City in 1955. The Browns went the opposite direction in 1954, going to Baltimore to become the Orioles. All three franchises enjoyed cities where they didn't have to share the baseball fans with a team in the other league, and all three played in bigger parks. The Brooklyn Dodgers and the New York Giants followed suit in 1958 by moving to Los Angeles and San Francisco, respectively. The last pre-Expansion team to migrate was the Washington Senators in 1960 when Cal Griffith shifted the family-owned team to Bloomington, Minnesota, a diplomatic move made to appease the fans in Minneapolis and St. Paul.

It seemed that all the best cities were covered by 1960, and Baseball would only have Chicago facing the problem of supporting two Major League teams. Attendance should rise, and with it, revenues.

But the owners weren't satisfied to make just a *little* more money, and Congress was so displeased about not having Major League Baseball in the nation's capital that there was a threat to withdraw its protective blanket of no anti-trust legislation. So someone came up with the idea of "Expansion".

New owners would have to pay the old owners a fee for getting into Major League Baseball, and in order to stock their rosters with experienced ballplayers, the new boys would have to buy the contracts of players from the established teams. Each team was allowed to protect 15 players on their 40-man rosters until one was drafted by an expansion team. Then the older club could protect two more players and only lose a maximum of eight men, gaining a million dollars in the process.

The established teams made out like bandits. They were able to pare off marginal veterans and their contracts from their rosters and payrolls, and at the same time protect good young prospects who, if they made the big club, would be getting paid less than the seasoned players they were replacing. It was a very lucrative deal for the owners. Expansion seemed to be the ideal way to bring in more profit.

Still, not all the owners were happy. The Braves and

A's moved again to greener pastures.

So to head off another wave of transfers, the Powers-that-be in Baseball opted for further expansion.

At the same time, someone else stumbled onto the idea that moving the franchise to another city wasn't the best answer to financial problems. All a team needed was a bigger and better playing facility. A lot of fans were staying away from baseball parks because most of the older stadia were located in old neighborhoods that offered no parking and were hard to get to from the suburbs. Atlanta got the Braves and Oakland got the A's for these very reasons. So instead of moving, all an owner had to do was *threaten* to move, and the city came up with a new stadium.

That wasn't true in all cases of new stadia being built, but even if the threat was never uttered, it was still there. Thus, the governments of Pittsburgh, Philadelphia, St. Louis, and Cincinnati responded quickly by erecting new sports complexes of one sort or another for their professional teams.

In Cincinnati, the Reds and football Bengals got Riverfront Stadium for a playground in 1970. It was good-bye to the centerfield terrace of Crosley Field and hello to symmetry and artificial turf. For a singles hitter like Pete, it was a bonanza.

As the All-Star Game approached, it was becoming apparent that Sparky Anderson was making a lot of correct decisions. The Reds were in front and appeared headed for a divisional crown. Also, Riverfront Stadium was ready for play.

For the last game at Crosley Field, the Reds faced

Juan Marichal and the San Francisco Giants. The game went into the bottom of the ninth tied. Pete slammed a triple, then scored on a sacrifice fly to make the Reds winners. Pete's three-bagger was the last hit at Crosley Field.

The next time the Reds played a home game they hosted the Atlanta Braves. Felix Millan singled in the top of the first to garner the honor of getting the first hit ever in the new stadium, but Pete singled off Pat Jarvis in the bottom of the first to get the first hit by a Cincinnati player at Riverfront. Pete was so excited about the new playing field that he went 4-for-5 that night.

Because Cincinnati had a new park, the All-Star Game was scheduled for Riverfront Stadium in 1970. The Reds were represented by Johnny Bench, Tony Perez, Jim Merritt, and Pete.

Pete wasn't a starter. He entered the game in the fifth inning, still looking for his first All-Star Game hit. He walked his first time up, then struck out the next two times. With the score tied, 4-4, in the bottom of the twelfth, Pete came to bat again, with two out and nobody on base. He singled to center. The Dodgers' Billy Grabarkewitz followed with a single, moving Pete to second. The Cubs' Jim Hickman came up and banged a single to center. Kansas City's Amos Otis fielded it cleanly and fired toward the plate. Pete rounded third, and Leo Durocher who was coaching there yelled, "You gotta go! You gotta go!" And Pete went.

The night before the game Pete had a couple of guests at his house. One was Cleveland catcher Ray Fosse. Pete entertained Fosse and pitcher Sam

McDowell, also of Cleveland, until after midnight. They were friends.

So who was blocking the plate when Pete headed down the baseline for home? Ray Fosse. The throw from Otis in center had Pete beaten by a few feet. Fosse caught it perfectly and turned to face what he thought would be a sliding runner. Instead of making his patented head-first slide, Pete opted to go in standing, crashing into Fosse as he did. The catcher crumpled in a heap, his glove coming off and the ball rolling free. The umpire signalled safe, and the National League won the game.

Some papers the next day made it look like Pete was deliberately trying to hurt Fosse. Pete continued to hear about it for the rest of the season, and to some fans he became a "dirty" player.

But when Pete made the exact same play a year later against the Dodgers' Duke Sims and Pete wound up on the short end, nothing was said about Sims trying to hurt Pete. Why? Because he wasn't trying to hurt Pete. He was merely doing his job, the same as Pete was when he slammed into Fosse. Pete was hurt in both collisions and missed a few games each time, but that's the chance he took. When you play all-out all the time, you have to expect to get hurt now and then.

Although some people kept bringing up the All-Star Game incident over and over during the remainder of the season, Pete put it past him and concentrated on winning a division title for Cincinnati. So did the rest of the Reds. By mid-September all their hard work paid off, and the Reds won the division by 14½ games.

The Pittsburgh Pirates put on a strong finish, typical of Danny Murtaugh teams, and won the East over the Cubs and Mets by 5 and 6 games, respectively. It was the Pirates' first title of any kind since 1960 when they won the NL pennant, then defeated the New York Yankees in the World Series.

The Pirates were no match for the Reds in the Championship Series. Cincinnati bounced the Bucs in three straight. Pete had three hits in 13 trips, scoring one run and batting in another.

Earl Weaver had been a mid-season replacement as manager of the Baltimore Orioles in 1968. He got the O's out of their doldrums immediately but not enough to catch the Detroit Tigers. In 1969, he had the Birds pick up right where they left off, and Baltimore won their division by a full 19 games over the Tigers. Then after knocking off the Minnesota Twins in three straight, they faced the New York Mets in the World Series. Baltimore won the first game, then the Mets swept the next four.

Embarrassed by their World Series defeat the year before, the Orioles were determined to repeat as champions of the American League in order to get another shot at the World Series. They won the East Division by 15 games over the Yankees, then wiped out the Twins again in three straight.

Offensively, both the Reds and Orioles had lots of punch and power. Both had good fielding. The Reds had adequate pitching, but Cincinnati didn't have three 20-game winners like Baltimore's Mike Cuellar (24-8), Dave McNally (24-9), and Jim Palmer (20-10).

The Orioles won the first three games by scores of 4-3, 6-5, and 9-3. They were four outs away from a sweep when Lee May hit a three-run homer that gave the Reds a 6-5 win in game four. Baltimore took game five, 9-3, and avenged their loss of a year earlier.

The Reds had nothing to be ashamed of. They had won 102 games in the regular season and four in post-season play. Johnny Bench led the league in homers with 45 and RBIs with 148. Jim Merritt won 20 games, and Gary Nolan won 18. Tony Perez had 40 round-trippers and 129 ribbies, and Lee May pounded out 34 homers with 94 RBIs. Perez hit .317; Bobby Tolan, .316; and Bernie Carbo, .306. Bench was named the National League's Most Valuable Player.

And Pete? He did all right. He tied the Cubs' Billy Williams for the league lead in hits with 205, his third straight 200-plus hits season and fifth in six years. He scored 120 runs and hit .316 in 159 games.

All things considered it was a pretty good season, and when Karolyn had a boy on November 16, it looked like a pretty good year. Pete named his son after himself, but Pete, Jr., quickly became "Googie" to Pete. On Thanksgiving Day, Pete had a lot to be thankful for.

On December 9, Pete went to the barbershop to get a haircut. The phone rang as the barber clipped away at Pete's coiffure. The call was for Pete.

"Your dad died," someone said.

"No, you mean my mom," said Pete. He was serious because his mother did have heart trouble.

"No, your dad," said the caller.

Shocked by what the caller was trying to tell him,

Pete finished the haircut, then went home still not consciously accepting the tragic news.

Later he learned that his father, who hadn't been sick a day in his life as the expression goes, had been at work when he became ill. He asked to go home and was given permission to do so. Instead of asking someone to drive him home, Harry took a crosstown bus. He collapsed on the stairs at home and died of a heart attack.

The guiding light of Pete's life was gone. Suddenly. At the age of 58. A young man in so many ways. Deprived of his leisure years that had been earned by so much hard work during a life dedicated to the happiness of everyone around him.

Pete's heart was broken. His father, who happened to also have been his best friend, was dead.

At the funeral, Pete was still numb, merely going through the motions of being alive. The minister stood and spoke, and Pete only heard bits and pieces. But one thing did stick in his mind. The preacher said, "You know, ladies and gentlemen, from the minute we're born we start to die."

Big Pete had said something similar to his son on more than one occasion, and Pete felt his father was speaking to him once again, only this time through the minister. And suddenly Pete realized that his father would be with him always.

14

From Around the World

One group of people who need a flag waved in their honor is the U.S. Postal Service employees.

The addresses on some letters were very strange. Some included to Mr. Hustle; to Pete; to Rose; to M.V.P.; to (a picture of a rose); Cincinnati, Ohio. Some had no zip, no street address, and a few even had no city name.

But the postal workers knew who the letters were for. Those guys brought bag after bag to the stadium for Pete. After his 3,000th hit, the amount of mail tripled. It came from all over the world: France, England, Germany, Japan, Australia, Africa, and Canada, to name a few. Some letters I couldn't read because they were written in a foreign language. I guessed at what most wanted, especially if there was a baseball card enclosed.

As the mail poured in, one of the local TV stations came to my house and videotaped us and the mail piled high in my livingroom. The interview appeared on the evening news. That only increased the amount of mail coming to Pete from fans in the local area.

After one of the ball games in September, I told Pete we were going to go abroad for three months and I could not do the mail until our return. Pete said it was all right and to put everything on hold until we returned. One of my daughters picked up all the mail bags at the stadium during our absence. When we returned, there were tens of thousands of letters to answer. We started again into answering his mail with Pete supplying us with thousands upon thousands of photos for us to send.

Dear Pete,

I was very sad when you did not get a hit against Atlanta on 8-1-78. At least Gene Garber could have challenged you and given you something to hit. This has been the greatest feat for baseball since the days of Mickey Mantle when he was an active player. I wish you could have slammed a home run against Garber in that 9th inning. You represent baseball at it's best. You are a genuine ball player, not a hot dog like some of the so called superstars who don't deserve Million dollar contracts. You are just great. Best of luck for the rest of the season, I hope you will hit in every game this last part of the year and also win the batting title. Thank you for what you have done for baseball, and for being Pete Rose, Mr. Hustle.

Sherie

8 years old.

The streak is over and Pete has started to hit again. It probably won't stretch into a long streak, but you can count on him trying for another one. Pete will give it his all.

Dear Pete 163

Hello there Pete: I've been wanting to write you al the time while your streak of lightning was going for you so well, but am going to write any way tonite. I want to congradulate you on your 44 hits and you showed them you meant what you said last nite about starting again tonite. I've followed the Reds for years on Radio.

I really like the way you play (any one can tell you really enjoy the game) and that Joe M. is next to in my books.

Now don't think I'm some "chick" trying to butter you up. I'm just a young (old) lady of 75 years who really enjoys her ball games. I am not too interested in other games only to watch where they are on and know where they stand.

Am glad you seldom play on Thurs. nite, thats my club nite.

 Just an interested Fan
  Fern

Another young at heart fan! "Old Father Time" takes his "coffee breaks" when he sees us enjoying something like baseball! (I should know, I'm slowly heading down that same lane, but act like a kid.)

Dear Mr. Rose,

My name is Barry, and I am a nineteen year old college Sophomore.

For many years you frustrated me to no end. For as long as I can remember, I've hated you as a ballplayer. I have no valid reason for my feelings, they just existed. High on my list was the time you scored the winning run in the All-Star game by cracking into Ray Fosse a few years ago. This incident made me really dislike you. Other times my hate reached peaks were

World Series in which you participated. Some times I rooted for the Reds, others I didn't but always there was an inner feeling of hatred towards you, for this, I wish to apologize and explain.

Although I'm from Maryland I've never been an Oriole fan. When I was small and very impressionable I rooted for the "other" teem to be different from my family and friends. In 1966 whin the Orioles won the World Series I was rooting for los Angles. In 1967 when the American league pennant was not decided until the last night I became a Boston Red Sox fan for the first time. Since that time I've been a diehard Red Sox fan to the end.

In 1975 my contempt for you reached its peak. You and the Reds had defeated my idols, Carl Yazstremski and the Bosox. It was probably the greatest Series ever played and I enjoyed it immensly, but I was close to tears when we lost and I raged inwordly at you.

I guess I was jealous of the attention you recieved for your hard work. At that time I thought you were a jack--- with on and off the field and a dirty ball player to boot! Since that time I've matured a great deal. Your recent hitting streak has been the height of my admiration of you. I've come to realize that you deserve everything you've ever achieved from your numerous awards and records to the national attention and acclaim. Above and beyond all this though I've come to respect and admire Pete Rose the man. You seem to humble now with all the attention you've received during and after your 44 game hitting streak its hard not to like you. Many times during the latter stages of your streak you showed little emotion, but I could tell how proud and happy you were, your pride shines through the darkest of nights and has given many young ball *players the courage and determination it takes to be a winner. No one wanted you to reach that magic number 56 more than I. Thats over now, though, and I've noticed that yesterday you and the Reds moved into first place. With your experienced ball club the near future looks bright for post season play. Best of luck in your pennant race. If the Reds should win remember I am a Boston fan and will probably be rooting against the Reds but no longer Pete Rose.*

It's been said that if you want something done you must do it yourself. this is true because no one else made me a Pete Rose fan except you. It was a long hard battle but you won using the same tools that have made you great. Hard work, pride, determination and Hustle. Many many congratulations on your record Streak of hits. May you enjoy many years of happiness and good fortune, both on and off the ball field. Thank you for entertaining myself along with all of America with your great attitude and playing ability.

Incidently because of the press I've heard that you have had family problems recently. My parents have been divorced for a year and a half now and I know what that is like. It tore my family apart. Realizing that these things are personal let me just say that I hope you are able to work things out. Few people deserve the love of their family more. My thoughts are with you in this endeavor also.

Thank you for your time
Sincerely,
Barry

It takes real guts to admit you are wrong and offer an apology! Pete Rose is a proud man, loyal to his fans and to his team. I am very proud to know the man!

Dear Mr. Rose,

Thank you for giving my children and all Reds a modern day hero. You have made "parenting" alot easier for many of us. It is very impressive to children that against all odds you were determined to succeed and did so well.

It is tough to be in the international spotlight and live up to the ideals that people, particularly children expect of you but you are doing a great job. Your influence on their attitude we'll be lasting tho' you may never know it.

Thank you for a job well done.

Mary

My children have all grown up, but I can see how it would be a little easier for children who watch T.V. so much these days, having an idol like Pete, watching him try to achieve his goals, and when he fails, he picks himself up and tries again. That gives them an incentive to do the same.

Anytime anyone wants something bad enough, *if* they work hard at it, they can usually succeed in getting it.

Dear Mr. Pete Rose,

Hope you'll be a '78 World Series Champion. Also a M.V.P. too, again.

P.S. Do you remember us? We are Japanese couple who joined August Reds Alert Weekend. And, happily, we've got pictured with you.

Thank you for nice memory with you.

Hiroko Hirano

Takami Hirano

A happy couple from Japan who wants to thank Pete for joining them at the Reds Alert Weekend.

Dear Pete,

I have enclosed a picture that my six year old boy drew of you after we went to see you at Shea Stadium. I thought you might get a kick out of it.

Just wanted to let you know that you've added a little excitement to an otherwise dismal summer for us Yankee fans. (Thank goodness things are picking up for our team.) You are the only person who could get us out to see the Mets, I'll tell you that. Anyway we saw you tie Tommy Holmes record and it was really fun. My son has since become a switch hitter and rarely goes out without his Reds helmet.

So I've sent you this picture at Damien's request and on my behalf I say I'm rooting for hit 56. I never believed I would see anyone beat that record. But I'll be cheering for you all the way.

Sincerely,
Michele

Someday, I sincerely hope that someone gets on a hitting streak like Pete's and goes on to beat all the records now standing. I hope Pete will do it, but if not, then it will have to be someone with his great hustle and desire!

Dear Pete:

We sincerely thank you for the enthusiasm excitement, and sheer pleasure which you have provided us over the past month and a half. We have watched and listened daily to your pro-

gress and it has meant a great deal to us, and added immeasurably to our lives.

True, you are "good" for baseball. But, the real truth is that your philosophy and joy are a pleasure to share, especially in an age where quality and competence are hard to find.

Keep on having fun. Thank you so much for the thrill of watching you.

With Respect,
Richard E.

The magic word is "fun". Pete enjoys playing ball. The enthusiasm and zeal that he inspires while he is playing touches his teammates and fans alike. It's magic, it brings pleasure to all.

Mr. Pete Rose:

This is not a hate letter, so please read on. I watched the game in Atlanta a few nights ago where your hitting stread was spoiled. I am a grandmother. My 2 grandsons 12 and 13 were also watching — we all continued to watch and listen as the interveiw followed on the air — live. The language was so foul — Surely, you have a vocabulary that could be used to express yourself without including such as you used — not once, but several times. There are still people in the world who do not approve and coming from a sports hero — Shame! It's too much to expect a reply.

Sincerely,
Mrs. Rieby

Granted, Pete should have watched his language; but he didn't know the mikes were turned on. He was upset, having missed hitting safely in the 45th game, frustrated at himself, and with all the tension that built up to this point, he just came unglued. I think all of us, when terribly upset, may say something that we wish we hadn't.

No one said Pete was a saint. Least of all, Pete!

Aloha Pete,

Like yourself, my first love is baseball and I've been taking my 3-year-old son in the backyard for about a year now. A good friend of mine sent me a 15-inch bat which is about perfect for him. But like all 3-year-olds, his span of interest is short.

Anyway, out of the blue last night, I got the surprise of my life when he approached me carrying a bat and ball. He put the ball down and, for a change, went into this crouching stance -- I never taught him that. I noticed he was holding the bat right, too.

Next thing he tells me is "Look daddy, Pete Rose." He must've picked it up from the T.V. -- we get the Atlanta cable here. It's remarkable, to me, that he picked up both your name and stance.

It's sort of silly, perhaps, but I just wanted to share what Chad did with you because I know how much Pete Jr. means to you.

Pass on my regards to an old friend, Mike Lum, for me and if you remember, might mention that he'll be an answer to a trivia question I've stored for use a few years from now. Mike's the only player to be in the same lineup as you and Hank Aaron on record-related nights. Mike was batting second when Aaron hit Nos. 714 and 715 and, of course, second the night you tied

Tommy Holmes.

Again, thanks for some "inspired help." Got to admit Chad picked a pretty good one as an example.

Aloha for now,
  Rod

Even at 3 they mimic Pete! All children are precious, and they do copy things. Maybe, with a lot of help from dad, you may have the next generation's version of Pete.

Dear Mr. Rose:

From the old school, I purposely didn't call you "Pete."

Just want to thank you for many weeks of cheer and excitement, the likes of which this country needs and hasn't had in many a moon. Thirty-six years ago may seem like a coon's age to a lot of people who followed your 44-hit streak, Mr. Rose, but at 62 years of age, I recall vividly Joe DiMaggio's 56-hit streak of 1941.

I was too short in those days to play baseball -- the same height as Patek these days -- so I took up track. Did the 100 in 10 seconds flat in 35 and 36, and that was good because I had a big mouth and still do!

Anyway, Mr. Rose, congratulations and thanks! You're a good guy, and God knows, with the press and a lot of the politicians today out to do this country in with criticisms of everything American, your recent (I say "recent," because you'll get in there again) streak brought a breath of good, old-fashioned American fresh air to this harassed nation.

Respectfully,
  Tom

Thank you for the last paragraph in your letter especially the line about good old American fresh air. How true!

Pete,

I would just like to send you my congradulations on your 44 game hitting streak. I can honestly say that I live and died with every at bat you had during your streak.

I am a distance runner in college trying to make it to the Olympic trials in 1980. During the summer I usually train at night, but during your streak, I ran in the heat of day to listen or watch you at night.

You are a great inspiration to me, as well as thousands of others and the 44 game steak couldn't have come to a more deserving person! Good luck in the 1978 World Series.

Your number one fan,
Tina

I think half the nation sat at their television sets each time Pete came to bat. It was an emotional time for the fans, too, because they wanted the streak to continue. I know, for I lived through the agony of it all the same as the other fans. Pete was upset the night that it ended, but the hustle in him shone through, and he was back there giving his 110% the next night. I hope you made it to the Olympics in 1980 with flying colors.

Dear Pete (Incredible Hulk) Rose,

You're my number one hero. I was really sad when you didn't hit 45. I thought I was going to cry. I've been a very big fan of your's and of the Cincinnati Reds for 2 years. I'm 13 years old and I'm a girl.

Were you disappointed when you didn't hit 45? Were you glad that all that pressure is over? I hope you don't retire! I don't know what I'd do if you do. You look to good and young to retire.

I think I'm in love with you. I also love all of the Cincinnati Reds including Sparky. But I've always liked you the best.

Love,
   your number one fan,
      Chris

You know, I think Pete is incredible too! And retire! Who Pete? It will be many years before Pete retires. He is having too much fun playing baseball.

Dear Mr. Rose,
   I am an avid San Fancisco Giants' fan, and quite naturally, I hate the Reds.

Concerning my support for baseball however, I idolize you. I was at the recent Giants-Reds game on June 20th, during which you gave me two moments of sublime satisfaction. Your attempt to score from third baseman only to be thrown out from leftfield by Terry Whitfield was indeed heroic. I must admit however, I quite honestly enjoyed watching the umpire raise his right hand and signaling you out. And then to top it all off, your protests were great, the way you created everything so visually. Thank you Mr. Rose, as we all enjoyed the show.

A moment earlier in the game though, epitomized the type of play which earned you the name "Charlie Hustle". On a short pop-up about half-way between third and home, you took three steps, then lunged, robbing another Giant hitter of a second chance at the plate. Throwing your body at the concrete like Astro-Turf, you were able to snare the ball before it had a chance to hit the ground.

Oddly enough, I cheered just as wildly for both plays. I realized that baseball is still a game played by human beings, who can become, and should become emotionally involved in the game. I've also learned though what it takes to be a winner, which you are Mr. Rose, and that is pride and hustle.

You had another opportunity recently to display that pride and hustle, and throughout you were magnificent. I am speaking of your recent 44-game hitting streak, and I would like to take this opportunity to congratualte you. During that span, you challenged third baseman to come in and guard against the bunt, even running the risk of having to accept a walk. Always, you hit for the good of the team, not for the sake of your own record.

The final scene to this 44-game scenario however, seemed somehow to dull the patina you had worked so hard to shine. Your comments to and concerning Gene Garber were discouraging, especially the comment that he was pitching as if it were the "World Series". Of all people Mr. Rose, you are the last I would have expected this type of comment from. Isn't that what professional baseball is all about, playing as if every game were the World Series?

You say Garber was unwilling to challenge you with a fastball, that he threw you changeups instead. Do you honestly feel you would have been proud of your streak had you continued at game 45 with a fastball. Mr. Rose, he did challenge you with his best, and he struck you out. Although I was saddened by the end of your magnificent streak, I was even more saddened by your comments following the contest.

Allow me to congratulate you once more on your streak, and someday I would like the chance to shake your hand and meet you personally.
 Sincerely,
  Christopher

Looking back now, Pete agrees. Gene Garber was doing his job.

Dear Mr. Rose,
 During this time which may be something of a let-down for you after ending your hitting streak, I just want you to know how much good you did this summer without even realizing it.
 My dad was very sick in the hospital (He died last Wednesday) and following the events of your hitting streak gave him much joy and put excitement and anticipation into a long day.
 I would imagine that what I am saying could probably be said by thousands of others! Again, I just thought you should know.
 Sincerely,
  Sister Mary, (A Reds fan — honest)

This letter helped Pete get over his disappointment about the streak coming to an end.

Dear Pete,
 While I'll admit I didn't want "Joe's" record broken I did want you to do it if it had to be done.
 Pete, you're not just a super-star. You're the best credit to your profession, and even more important the type of guy I

hope my son turns out to be.
Sincerely yours,
Bill

If you are a true Joe Dimaggio fan, I can see how you feel about his streak remaining in the books.

Dear Pete:
You gave us all an incredible ride for 44 games. We're truly sorry it had to end, but thank you very much for the lift.
Best wishes for continued success.
Cordially,
THE HARLEM GLOBETROTTERS, INC.

Dear Mr. Pete Rose,
I was listening to the radio here in Germany every morning to hear if you kept your hitting streak going. I was very saddened to hear your streak was broken at 44 in Atlanta.
In my book your as great or greater than Joe DiMaggio even if you had neven gotten as close to him as you did. Your the Greatest!
I have always been a fan of the Reds, and your one of the biggest reasons. Good luck on your next try.
Sincerely yours,
Richard

Hi Pete,
Back in 1952, Ty Cobb wrote an article for LIFE *magazine where his said,"Nobody in the major leagues today — not even Jackie Robinson, Sam Jethro or Minnie Minoso — is a first-class baserunner." It's a shame Ty Cobb never saw Pete*

Rose play that game.
   Good luck,
    Mike

Dear Pete:
   You are a living symbol of what athletes and athletics cn be
and an example of dedication and commitment that I point to
for my students and my children.
   If you need any consolation . . . and you shouldn't . . .
perhaps it can come from the fact that a "rookie" had a hand in
stopping you at 44 who apparently considered it more of a
privilege to pitch to you than to be a part of holding you
hitless. Good luck always from a fan in Michigan.
   Sincerely,
    Jim

   A school principal wrote this to Pete. Dedication and
commitment can make everyone improve and secure
the fulfillment of their goals, not just athletes. Thanks
for your best wishes for Pete.

Hi, Pete,
   How are you doing? When I was in the U.S.A., I was always
rooting for you and I am now, too. I went to the Candlestick
park — which you hate most — several times to see your
playing.
   I hope that 1978 will be the year that you get the batting
champion title and the Big Red Machine is the World Cham-
pion. I'm keeping my fingers crossed in Japan that those two
things come true.
   Katsuya

Dear Pete   **177**

Another fan from Japan. Too bad the "Reds" didn't even win their division in 1978.

Dear Pete,

    As for your remarks about Garber, would you really expect him not to try and get you out or to just groove it for you? Answer this one; suppose McWilliams had a no-hitter, or a perfect game going with a 12 run lead, and you were the last batter, since your team could probably not win, would you try not to get a hit?

    I hope that your 4 for 5 Wednesday starts a new streak, and if anyone playing today can make a run at 56, it will be you.

    Sincerely,
    Jim

A very good point made here about Garber. The pitcher did what he was suppose to do and yes, Pete Rose would try to get a hit, no matter if it was a perfect game or a no hitter.

Pete,

    I guess the first time I really had any feelings about you was when you had that incident with Bud Harrelson. I'm a Met fan so naturally, I hated you. However, I've grown in the last few years and I've come to like you very much. I guess it started when I found that we both have the same birthday. I'm wondering if you chose 14 as your because it's you birth date.

    I wasn't able to follow the beginning of your streak, but I did see the end and I went to the game at Shea when you broke the National League (modern) record. It must have felt good to get cheers from the New York fans.

Also, for you to answer all your mail it must take a lot of stamps, so I've included one along with my appreciation.

Ken

Pete was elated when the fans from New York cheered him! Thanks for sending the stamp and best wishes to you.

Dear Pete,

You are looking at your two most ardent fans . . . the one on the left being the next Pete Rose I hope. He may not be as cute, but he's sweet!

I could lie and tell you I'm writing this for my 8 year old son, but this is strictly from a 34 year old mom who adores you. Admittedly, a gal who reads the box scores before fixing the kids breakfast, I probably wouldn't be writing this.

I've never written to total stranger other than Santa Claus, so this a little awkward for me.

You were the inspiration for the Khoury League team I helped coach this year. I used to tell them about "Charlie Hustle" and how you never gave up or stopped trying just because the Reds were behind. We finished first. You're a wonderful and positive inspiration and a great hero for kids today, and as a parent, I'm grateful.

My birthday is next month during your series back in Atlanta and I'm trying to talk my husband into letting me fly up to watch you stick it to Gene Garber. Anyway, I hope I can see you in Atlanta, if not when I see you on T.V. I'll be praying for you and cheering you on.

Barbara

Dear Pete 179

Great success in your coaching of the youngsters in your area, may you come in first every year.

Pete's dedication to baseball and his all out hustle and enthusiasm do tend to inspire the youngsters to copy his batting stance, his base running, and his hitting. The children try to be miniature Pete Roses which will give us, a hustling, energetic group of ballplayers of superb quality in the future.

Dear Pete,

I just read your article in Sports Illustrated and your statement about how hustle was responsible for everything you had obtained. It is certainly a pleasure to hear a man with you great ability give credit to hard work and desire, rather than natural ability.

As a high school coach, I am concerned that the attitude of today's youth does not vary from the overall goals of a good atheletic program. I try to teach those values and to hold their heads high; whether they got their 3000th hit or struck out in the sand lot game down the street. I simply wanted to thank you for making my day and job a little brighter.

Yours Truly,
Allen

Pete is sincere when he says work, desire, and hustle are what is required to make goals happen. It is nice to hear someone say Pete's attitude helps make their days and jobs a little easier.

15

The Big Red Machine

Baseball has had its memorable teams over the years. Everyone of them had its mark of distinction. Some were a one-year phenomenon, others a dynasty. The Cincinnati Reds of the 1970s fit both descriptions.

From 1906 to 1910, the Chicago Cubs won four National League pennants and two World Series under Frank Chance of Tinker-to-Evers-to-Chance. Miller Huggins' New York Yankees of the 1920s with their "Murderers Row" dominated the American League with six pennants in eight years, capping their reign by sweeping Pittsburgh and St. Louis respectively in the 1927 and 1928 World Series. The Cardinals of late 20s and early 30s had the "Gas House Gang" that won five National League pennants and three world titles in nine years. Connie Mack's Philadelphia Athletics of 1929-1931 were thought to be even better than the Yankees before them. But the Great Depression forced Mack to break up his team, and the A's dynasty was never really established.

Then 1936 came along, and the Yankees started what has to be the greatest dynasty in sports history. New York won 22 AL flags in 29 years, capturing the World Series 16 times. From 1949 through 1953, Casey Stengel managed the Yanks to five straight world titles, breaking the record set by John McCarthy who directed the same Yankees to victory in the World Series from 1936 through 1939.

It was thought in the late 1960s that the word dynasty would never again be applied to Major League baseball teams. The rules had been changed whereby the rich, such as the Yankees, could no longer sign the best talent in the country or buy it from the poorer teams. The "draft" had been installed in 1965, and the lesser teams were given first crack at signing young players. Network television revenue was being shared by the teams, and this helped financially pressed franchises to meet salary demands by star players. For one team to become predominant in its league, skillful management would be needed.

Bob Howsam had taken over the position of general manager of the Cincinnati Reds in 1967. The stars that had won the pennant in 1961 were almost all gone, and they had to be replaced. Immediately, he began making several important trades to improve his ball club. But trading isn't enough. In order to get something, you have to give up something. And once you've exhausted your tradeable personnel on the major league level you have to dip into your minor league talent. The Reds' GM was averse to doing that.

Already, the Cincinnati farm system had produced

Pete Rose, Tommy Helms, Tony Perez, Tommy Harper, Chico Ruiz, Leo Cardenas, Johnny Bench, Gary Nolan, and Lee May. And there was more talent down in the minors as the 1970 season began. Pitchers Wayne Simpson and Don Gullett and outfielders Hal McRae and Bernie Carbo were waiting for their chance to help the big club.

Although the Reds had won the division and the pennant in 1970, Sparky Anderson and Howsam were still not satisfied with the make-up of the team.

The San Francisco Giants, as always, had an abundance of outfielders but were lacking a good defensive shortstop. Some weeks into the season Howsam made them an offer they couldn't refuse. He sent them shortstop Frank Duffy for a skinny leftfielder with an anemic bat. For good measure and so the Giants wouldn't feel cheated, he threw pitcher Vern Geishert into the deal. Cincinnati got George Foster.

The 1971 campaign was a lesson in futility for the Reds. Only Lee May among the regulars had a better season than he had in 1970. Pitcher Don Gullett had a full season and went 16-6 compared to the partial year record of 5-2 in 1970. Clay Carroll was still just as tough coming out of the bullpen. Everyone else on the team slipped in performance, including Pete, whose numbers dropped in almost every category. He hit .304 with 192 hits, 27 doubles, 4 triples, 13 homers, and 44 RBIs. He had 17 fewer trips to the plate, but more importantly, he scored 24 fewer runs than he did in 1970. His statistics didn't fall off as much as others', but they show why the Reds finished in a tie for fourth, 11 games behind the Giants, and four games under .500.

Adding to the Reds' miseries was a plague of injuries. Bobby Tolan, Wayne Simpson, and Jim Merritt were the most notable absentees from the lineup cards of Sparky Anderson.

Pete and the rest of the Cincinnati team watched the Pittsburgh Pirates, winners in the East by seven games over St. Louis, pound the hurting Giants into submission in the league Championship Series, losing the first game then winning the next three.

The Pirates then faced Baltimore, who had won its third straight American League crown by whipping Oakland in three games. The O's were heavily favored to win the World Series, and after taking the first two games, odds were they would sweep Pittsburgh in four. The Orioles had four 20-game winners in Mike Cuellar, Dave McNally, Jim Palmer, and Pat Dobson, and they had Frank Robinson and Brooks Robinson, not to mention Dave Johnson, Don Buford, and Boog Powell. Power and pitching usually rule in a short series, but some of the Pirates hadn't heard that before.

The Pirates had the hitting to compete, but their pitching had been suspect throughout all of 1971. Someone forgot to tell the Orioles as pitcher Steve Blass put on a remarkable performance, beating the Orioles, 5-1, on a three-hitter in Game 3, then besting them, 2-1, on a four-hitter in Game Seven. Nelson Briles threw a two-hit shutout in Game 5, and rookie Bruce Kison came on in the first inning of Game 4 to halt a Baltimore barrage, then shut down the Orioles for the next six innings, before giving way to ace reliever

Dave Giusti who finished off the Birds.

Roberto Clemente and Bob Robertson hit two home-runs each in the last five games, and Clemente hit .414 for the Series.

Pete gained some satisfaction out of watching the Bucs do in the Orioles, but he itched to get back into the World Series himself. So did the rest of the Reds and general manager Bob Howsam.

Howsam went on a trading expedition in November, and he found a lot of teams willing to take a few of his stars off his hands but very few who wanted to give up any quality players. The Reds needed speed, a little more defense, and a lot of pitching. Howsam got it all from the Houston Astros. The Astros wanted some power. They got it. Howsam gave up Lee May and Tommy Helms, but he got Joe Morgan, Denis Menke, Cesar Geronimo, and Jack Billingham. Morgan brought speed to the club; Menke would allow Tony Perez to move to first from third, Geronimo would be a good defensive substitute for Bobby Tolan in centerfield, and Billingham would be the strong arm needed in the starting rotation. For the bullpen, Howsam sent right-hander Wayne Granger to Minnesota for portsider Tom Hall.

The 1972 season didn't start on time. The players went on strike April 1 and stayed out for two weeks. But when the campaign did begin, the Reds put it into high gear and roared through the season.

Every move Bob Howsam had made the year before seemed to pay off. Jack Billingham was only 12-12, but he kept the Reds in a lot of games, enough for the bullpen to hold the opposition while the hitters put the winning run across in the late innings. Hall, Carroll, and Pedro Borbon combined for a 24-8 record with 56 saves. Second-year pitcher Ross Grimsley went 14-8, and Don Gullett was 15-5 to lead the league in winning percentage.

The return of Bobby Tolan to the regular lineup, Denis Menke at third, and Cesar Geronimo in right improved the defense. But the biggest improvement in the team was a 5'7", 150-pound dynamo named Joseph Leonard Morgan. With Pete sandwiched between Morgan and Tolan at the head of the hitting order, the RBI men in the middle of lineup were bound to have good years.

And they did. Johnny Bench hit 40 homers and knocked in 125 runs, leading the league in both categories. Tony Perez had 21 roundtrippers and 90 RBIs. Tolan had 82 RBIs. Morgan, free at last from the confines of the Astrodome, pounded out 16 homers with 73 RBIs, but more important than power was his speed. Little Joe had 161 hits and 115 walks and scored a league leading 122 runs. A lot of them were the direct result of his 58 stolen bases.

Pete had an average year for him. He hit .307 with a league-leading 198 hits, 31 doubles, 11 triples, 6 homers, and 57 RBIs. For the first time in six years he didn't make the All-Star game, being selected but unable to play due to injury.

The Pirates won the NL East again, beating out the Cubs by 11 games. Steve Blass picked up where he had left off in the 1971 World Series and won 19 games with a 2.49 ERA. Aging Roberto Clemente and Al Oliver each hit .312, and Willie Stargell pounded out 33 home-runs and 112 RBIs.

The 1972 NL Championship Series promised to be the best ever in the short history of that post-season playoff, and it was.

Blass beat the Reds in the first game at Pittsburgh, 5-1, Cincinnati's only run coming off the bat of Joe Morgan as he homered in the first inning.

The second game went to the Reds, 5-3, as the Big Red Machine went to work on Pittsburgh starter Bob Moose in the very first inning. The Reds' first five batters hit safeties, chasing the big pitcher to the showers and scoring four runs in the top of the first. The Pirates chipped away with single tallies in each of the fourth, fifth, and sixth innings. Tom Hall relieved Jack Billingham in the fifth and was the winning pitcher. Morgan added an insurance run in the eighth with his second homer of the series.

The series moved to Cincinnati for the third game, and the Pirates rallied from 2-0 deficit to win 3-2. Manny Sanguillen homered for the Bucs' first run, then drove home the winner in the eighth off Clay Carroll.

Ross Grimsley had the duty of keeping the Reds in contention for the pennant in the fourth game and rose to the occasion by beating Pittsburgh, 7-1, with a two-hitter, one of those being a homer by Clemente. The win pushed the series to a fifth game, the first time in the history of the NL Championship Series that five games were needed to determine the pennant winner.

Pirates' manager Bill Virdon went with the ace of his

staff Steve Blass, and Sparky Anderson chose Don Gullett to start the deciding game. Pittsburgh scored twice in the second to take an early lead, and the Reds got one back in the third. The Pirates made it 3-1 in the fourth, and Cesar Geronimo tightened the gap to 3-2 in the fifth with a homer. The score stayed the same until the bottom of the ninth. Virdon brought in his ace reliever Dave Giusti to start the last inning. Johnny Bench was leading off, and the Cincinnati catcher proved he was a gamer by stroking a four-bagger and tying the game at 3-all. Tony Perez and Denis Menke followed with singles, and Virdon had seen enough of Giusti. He brought in Bob Moose who promptly got two outs, but with George Foster on third and Hal McRae at bat, Moose uncorked a wild pitch to let Foster cross the plate with the winning run. The Reds were in the World Series for the second time in three years.

Charles O. Finley had moved the Athletics from Kansas City to foggy California in 1968. The A's had the makings of pretty fair team when they arrived in Oakland. Already on the team were Bert Campaneris at shortstop, Sal Bando at third, Reggie Jackson in right, Joe Rudi in left, Dick Green at second, and Dave Duncan behind the plate, and the pitching staff had Jim "Catfish" Hunter and Johnny "Blue Moon" Odom. First class reliever Rollie Fingers came up to the big club in 1969; Vida Blue became a regular starter in 1971; and slugging first sacker Mike Epstein came in a trade with Washington in 1971. Oakland finished sixth in the 10-team AL in 1968, second in the AL West in 1969, second in 1970, and won the division in 1971 only to lose in the Championship Series to Baltimore. Manager Dick Williams who had taken over the reins in '71 felt he needed one more solid pitcher to make it to the World Series, so the A's traded centerfielder Rick Monday, the first player ever taken in the draft, to the Chicago Cubs for lefty Kenny Holtzman. As the strike-shortened '72 season began, Williams was sure he had all the pieces to the puzzle.

Oakland started slow but finished strong, winning their division by 5½ games over the Chicago White Sox. The A's met the Detroit Tigers of fiery manager Billy Martin in the Championship Series, and every game featured outstanding pitching. The A's won the first two games in Oakland, then the Tigers took the next two in Detroit. Going into the fifth game, both teams knew the winner would have to face Cincinnati's Big Red Machine in the World Series. Blue Moon Odom gave up a run in the first inning, but Oakland tied it in the second. Gene Tenace singled home George Hendrick in the fourth to put the A's ahead, 2-1. Vida Blue replaced Odom in the sixth and held the Tigers scoreless the rest of the way as the A's won, 2-1.

In their Championship Series against Pittsburgh, the Reds had only hit .253 as a team which was only slightly better than the .251 they had hit during the regular season. Johnny Bench hit .333 against the Pirates, and Pete hit .450 with 9 hits in 20 at-bats. The rest of the team had a meager 27 hits in 128 official trips to the plate. Cincinnati did have 4 homers in five games which was what they averaged during the season. The Big Red Machine appeared to be ready to crush Oakland.

Dick Williams has always been considered one of Baseball's craftiest managers, and in the 1972 World Series he showed why. He chose Kenny Holtzman, the former National Leaguer, to start the opening game in Cincinnati. Holtzman had always been tough on the Reds, and in one of his last appearances against the Reds in Cincinnati in 1971 he had beaten the Reds, 1-0, with a no-hitter. He held the Reds to two runs over five innings. Meanwhile, Gary Nolan was checking the A's as best he could, making only two mistakes, both gopher balls to unheralded back-up catcher Gene Tenace who set a World Series record by homering his first two times up. Rollie Fingers relieved Holtzman in the sixth, and Vida Blue came on in the seventh to gain the save as Oakland won the first game, 3-2.

Catfish Hunter held the Reds scoreless until the ninth in the second game but was pulled with two out in the final inning as the Reds mounted a threat, narrowing the score to 2-1. Fingers got the last out, and Oakland headed home with 2-0 lead in games.

In the third game, Jack Billingham and Clay Carroll combined for a three-hit shutout, and Tony Perez scored the only run of the contest in the seventh inning on a single by Cesar Geronimo.

Sparky Anderson called on Don Gullett to pitch the fourth game, and the lefthander responded by holding Oakland to one run in seven innings. The Reds pushed a pair of tallies across the plate in the eighth to take a 2-1 lead into the ninth. Pedro Borbon had relieved Gullett in the eighth and held Oakland scoreless. With one out in the ninth, the A's rallied off Carroll, getting four straight singles and two runs to win, 3-2, and take a 3-1 lead in games.

With their backs to the wall, the Reds looked to their captain in Game Five for the leadership he had provided all year long. Pete responded by taking Catfish Hunter's first pitch of the game downtown, giving the Reds an early 1-0 lead. Gene Tenace socked his fourth homer of the Series in the second with two on, and Oakland led 3-1. The Reds made it 3-2 in the fourth, only to have the A's go up 4-2 in the bottom of the inning. Another run in the fifth brought Cincinnati within one again, and one more in the eighth tied it. Pete singled home a teammate in the ninth to give the Reds their second win, 5-4.

Game Six was back in Cincinnati, and the Reds, who had lost seven straight World Series games at home, responded to homecooking by belting Oakland, 8-1. Bench hit his only homer of the Series in the contest, and Ross Grimsley picked up his second win in relief. Bobby Tolan and Cesar Geronimo each had two RBIs.

Jack Billingham, who had a win in Game Three and a save in Game Five, started for the Reds, and Dick Williams tabbed Odom to start for Oakland. Once more it was a pitchers' game. Oakland scored in the first, and the Reds tied it in the fifth. The A's got to Borbon in the sixth for a pair of runs to go up 3-1. Cincinnati could only muster one more tally in the eighth, and A's held on in the ninth to win, 3-2, and take the World Series.

Pete was disappointed in himself for only hitting .214 in the Series, going 6-for-28. Although he had given every pitch and every play his usual 110%, he felt he

Dear Pete   **191**

had let his team down. More than ever he wanted a new season to begin, just to atone for his unequal performance in the 1972 World Series.

Sparky Anderson and Bob Howsam felt they had a pretty solid team as they went into spring training 1973. Hal McRae and Wayne Simpson had been traded to Kansas City for Richie Scheinblum and Roger Nelson. Both Scheinblum and Nelson were coming off their best seasons in the Major Leagues. Just before the season started Howsam added journeyman outfielder Andy Kosco and utility infielder Phil Gagliano to the roster in a trade with Boston. Anderson liked the looks of young Dan Driessen during training camp and added the infielder to the opening day roster.

The season was hardly underway, it seemed, when Nelson went down with an injury and Scheinblum was shipped off to California. The Reds were struggling, and once again the bugaboo seemed to be injuries to the pitching staff.

In June Howsam swung a deal that had a direct bearing on the pennant race. He picked up 5'8" Fred Norman, a lefthanded pitcher, from the San Diego Padres for two no-name players. Norman had a 1-7 record for the Padres in 12 starts that season, and his record before 1973 was 14-28. But Norman had never played for a decent team. With the Big Red Machine behind him, Norman went on to post a 12-6 mark with a 3.30 ERA for the Reds.

The Reds had a solid starting rotation of Billingham, Grimsley, Gullett, and Norman down the stretch, and a bullpen of Borbon, Hall, and Carroll. The seven of them combined to win 89 of the club's 99 victories, with Billingham missing a 20-win season by only one victory, going 19-10. Gullett was 18-8; Grimsley, 13-10; Hall, 8-5, with 8 saves; Borbon, 11-4, with 14 saves; and Carroll, 8-8, with 14 saves.

The Cincinnati staff was only the fourth best in the National League, but the team led the league in the most important category of all. They outscored their opponents by 120 runs.

The Los Angeles Dodgers kept the pressure on the Reds all the way, but Cincinnati held them off to win the division by 3½ games.

Two arguments came into play concerning the divisional race in the NL East as the last week of the season began. With five teams still very much in contention and none of them more than a few games over the .500 mark with ten days to go, fans were divided over the strength of the division as a whole. Were the teams in the East so strong that not one or two of them could dominate the others? Or was the division that weak? Those questions were still unanswered as the regular season came to an end with the New York Mets on top by a game and a half over the St. Louis Cardinals, 2½ over the Pirates, 3½ over Montreal, and 5 over Chicago. The number of games separating the teams was a good argument in favor of the strength of the division, but the fact that the Mets finished with an 82-79 record and St. Louis was the only other .500 team at 81-81 supported the contention that the NL East was made up of a bunch of weak sisters.

Cincinnati won 17 more games than the Mets during

the regular season, and the Reds were odds-on favorites to sweep the Mets in the Championship Series. The boys from Cincy were the Big Red Machine. What were the Mets? Their leading hitter was Felix Millan at .290; John Milner led them with 23 homers; Rusty Staub was tops with 76 RBIs; they had a team batting average of only .246; and their pitching was only slightly better than the Reds' staff. The playoffs appeared to be a real mismatch on paper.

The Mets did have one thing in their favor, an intangible that no one ever looks at when trying to prognosticate a winner. New York had a history of miracles, whether those miracles were performed by the old New York Giants at Coogan's Bluff (witness Bobby Thomson's ninth inning, two-out, three-run homer to beat the Dodgers in a three-game playoff in 1951); the Brooklyn Dodgers; the New York Jets of the National Football League (witness Joe Namath and the Jets upsetting the heavily favored Baltimore Colts in Super Bowl III); the New York Knicks; or those "Amazin' Mets" of 1969 who overcame the Cubs 9½ game lead in August to win the NL East, then the pennant, then the World Series by defeating the heavily favored Baltimore Orioles.

"Tom Terrific" Seaver pitched the opening game for the Mets in Cincinnati. The Reds put Jack Billingham on the mound. Seaver was his usual magnificent self for seven innings, holding the Reds scoreless. Billingham had his stuff, too, as he only allowed the Mets one run through eight. Then Pete stepped to the plate and parked a Seaver fastball in the stands to tie the game at 1-all going into the ninth. Pedro Borbon put down a

Mets' threat in the ninth, then Johnny Bench crashed a four-bagger in the bottom of the inning to give Cincinnati the win.

The second game was another pitching duel until the ninth inning. Jon Matlack went the distance for New York, shutting out the Reds on two hits. The score was only 1-0 until the last inning when the Mets scored four times to put the game away, 5-0.

Game Three in New York was all Mets. Lefty Jerry Koosman took the hill for the Mets and held the Reds to a pair of tallies, while his teammates jumped all over Ross Grimsley, Tom Hall, and Dave Tomlin for 9 runs in the first four innings. The Mets were up 2-1 in games. The Mets won, 9-2, but the third game of the 1973 National League Championship Series will be remembered more for a play that didn't show up in the box score.

Pete was on first. A grounder was hit to second. Millan scooped up the ball and tossed it to Bud Harrelson who tagged the base and made the throw to first to complete the doubleplay. As always, Pete was giving the play his best. Knowing he was out at second, he did what every runner is supposed to do in that situation; he tried to break up the doubleplay by sliding at the shortstop. Harrelson took offense to Pete's attempt to up-end him and started toward Pete with anger in his eyes as soon as he had made the throw to first. Pete has never been one to back down. He headed toward Harrelson and threw a punch, the first punch, the one every good fighter gets in. He and Harrelson went down in a heap, and both benches raced onto the

Dear Pete   **195**

field. A brawl ensued. Players were ejected and order was finally restored.

Pete went out to leftfield in the bottom of the inning, and the New York fans began throwing debris at him. Fearing a forfeit, several Mets' players ran out to calm the fans and did so. The game progressed without further incident, but Harrelson had to have medical attention for a cut that Pete had inflicted on him.

Said Pete of the affair: "I'm not sorry about anything. Me sliding hard into Harrelson trying to break up a doubleplay was baseball the way it's supposed to be played. I'm no damn little girl out there. I'm supposed to give the fans their money's worth and play hard and try to bust up doublepays — and shortstops."

Harrelson had a different view. "I didn't think it was a clean play at the time. It was a big game; a competitive atmosphere. He was all fired up. He was always doing things to fire up his team. He didn't want to apologize. He probably felt, in his mind, he didn't have to apologize. He likes to play hard. He hit me after the play was over."

The air over Flushing Meadows was supercharged as Game Four got underway. The New York media had done its usual hatchet job, blaming Pete for the fight the previous day and practically calling for a lynch mob to string him up from a light tower at Shea Stadium. One thing is for sure: the Mets' fans were definitely in that kind of mood when Pete stepped to the plate for the first time that day and when he walked out to leftfield in the bottom of the first.

Sparky Anderson started Freddie Norman for the

Reds, and Yogi Berra countered with lefty George Stone who had posted a 12-3 mark with a 2.80 ERA during the regular season. Norman gave up a solo run in the third, and Stone held the Reds down until the seventh when Tony Perez smacked a round-tripper to tie the game. The contest went into extra innings. Tug McGraw held the Reds scoreless until he was lifted for a pinchhitter in the bottom of the eleventh. Don Gullett picked up for Norman in the sixth and pitched four shutout innings before giving way to Clay Carroll who did likewise for two frames. Then the villain of October 8, Pete Rose, came to bat in the twelfth with big right-hander Harry Parker on the mound for the Mets. Parker put one in Pete's power zone, and Pete reciprocated by sending it into the stands. Borbon set down the Mets in the bottom of the inning, and the series was tied at two games apiece.

It all came down to one game, and both teams put their best on the field. Berra started Seaver, and Anderson countered with Billingham. The Cincinnati ace didn't have his usual stuff, and Seaver was less than spectacular. New York scored twice in the first, but the Reds came back with single tallies in the third and fifth to tie the game at 2-all through 4½ innings. Then the roof caved in. Billingham couldn't get anyone out in the fifth and was replaced by Gullett who had the same problem. Clay Carroll came in to put out the fire, but he was too late. The Mets put four runs across the plate to take a 6-2 lead. They added one more in the sixth, and Seaver had a five-run lead, which was more than he needed. The Reds mounted a minor threat in the ninth but failed to score as McGraw got the last two outs to put the Mets in the World Series against Oakland.

The Athletics won their second straight pennant by coming back from a 2-0 deficit in games to defeat the Baltimore Orioles for the right to play the Mets and the New York miracle.

The Mets and A's split the first two games in Oakland and the first two games in New York. Jerry Koosman and Tug McGraw shutout Oakland in Game Five to take a 3-2 lead back to Oakland, but the A's showed their stuff by winning the final two games behind Jim Hunter and Kenny Holtzman to take the World Series for the second year in a row. The Mets had run out of miracles.

For Pete, 1973 was a most memorable year in his career. The only thing that tarnished his personal triumphs was the fact the Reds were not World Champs. He set some awesome figures in his career statistics. He won the batting title by 18 points, hitting .338 to the Houston Astros' Cesar Cedeno's .320. He had 680 official trips to the plate; scored 115 runs; set a Cincinnati club record with 230 hits; pounded out 36 two-basehits, 8 triples, and 5 homers; and knocked in 64 runs. To cap it all, the sportswriters around the National League had the good sense to name him the circuit's Most Valuable Player.

Pete also took one more step toward Baseball immortality on June 20, 1973. The Reds were in San Francisco to play the Giants. Ron Bryant was on the mound for Frisco when Pete rapped out the 2,000th hit of his career.

Believing a team that stands pat becomes stagnant, Bob Howsam went to the trading floor again. He sent Bobby Tolan and Dave Tomlin to San Diego for pitcher Clay Kirby and picked up outfielder Merv Rettenmund and utility infielder Junior Kennedy from Baltimore for Ross Grimsley. In spring training he purchased the contract of outfielder Terry Crowley from Texas.

After a good showing in September the year before, Ken Griffey stuck with the big club, and as the year progressed, George Foster started making his mark as a Cincinnati regular. Dan Driessen became the regular thirdbaseman.

On paper the Reds appeared to be stronger than ever. The pitching staff wasn't much different, and the regular lineup was still awesome with Johnny Bench behind the plate, Tony Perez on first, Joe Morgan at second, Dave Concepcion at short, Driessen at third, Cesar Geronimo in right, Rettenmund and Griffey then Foster and Griffey platooning in center, and Pete in left. They appeared unbeatable.

The Los Angeles Dodgers and their great manager Walter Alston had other ideas. The Bums had their usual array of pitching talent, but they also had an infield that was just coming into its own. Steve Garvey, Davey Lopes, Bill Russell, and Ron Cey around the horn were playing their first year together as a unit. They would remain the regulars for eight years, longer than any other infielding quartet in the history of Major League Baseball. LA also made one very important acquisition during the winter trading season. They sent lefthanded pitcher Claude Osteen to Houston for

"The Toy Cannon", Jimmy Wynn. This gave them the big power-hitter they had lacked the year before when they finished second to the Reds.

It was a two-team race for the NL West Division title from the very start. The Reds got off to a so-so start, and the Dodgers got on a roll early. By the All-Star Game, Cincinnati was playing catchup ball. They never could quite overtake Los Angeles and were finally eliminated on October 2 in Atlanta.

Pete had an off year. Although he may never admit it, part of the reason may be a major distraction he had off the field. Before spring training even began, Pete signed a contract with publishing company Prentice-Hall to write a diary-type book in conjunction with sportswriter Bob Hertzel of the Cincinnati *Enquirer*. The final product was titled *Charlie Hustle*. Although it's quite obvious from the book that Pete was having fun doing his story of the 1974 season, it showed that he wasn't concentrating as hard on the game as he normally does. The book was far from a literary success. Pete's remarks were for the most part entertaining, but his co-author and publisher failed to do him justice, making Pete appear to be something akin to an unlettered bozo by not editing out some statements and phrases that were often repetitious and redundant and by allowing him to ramble on too frequently.

Pete suffered through more than one slump during the 1974 season, and it is clear from his writing in *Charlie Hustle* that his thinking processes were being divided between his obligation to his publisher and his duty to his team. He finished the season with a sub-par

.284 average with 185 hits, his lowest total since getting 176 hits in 1967. It also broke his string of nine consecutive seasons of hitting over .300. Had he hit .300 that year he would have had 15 straight seasons over that mark at the end of the decade.

Although the Reds won 98 games in 1974, Cincinnati finished four games behind the Dodgers. Los Angeles blew out Pittsburgh in the Championship Series in four games, then faced Oakland in the first all West Coast World Series.

The A's were the first team since the New York Yankees to win three straight American League flags. The Yanks won five straight from 1960 through 1964. Oakland was also trying to capture its third consecutive World Series title, last achieved by the Yankees when they won five in a row from 1949 through 1953.

The Series started like most of the recent October Classics. Oakland's Kenny Holtzman and Rollie Fingers outdueled LA's Andy Messersmith and Mike Marshall to win, 3-2, in Los Angeles. The Dodgers' Don Sutton and Marshall came back in Game Two to beat Vida Blue and Blue Moon Odom by the same score. Game Three in Oakland went to Catfish Hunter and Fingers over four Dodger throwers, again by the score of 3-2. The A's broke the mold in Game Four by backing Holtzman with five runs to win, 5-2. Joe Rudi hit a seventh inning homer in Game Five to give the A's their third straight title, and Rollie Fingers picked up his fourth save of the Series to set an unbeatable record.

Winter came and it was trading season again. But a funny thing happened. Or didn't happen. Bob Howsam wasn't in the market.

Sparky Anderson had the players, the same players that had finished the season before. All he need was for everyone to stay healthy.

They did for the most part.

The 1975 Cincinnati Reds were incredible. They won 108 games and finished 20 games in front of the Dodgers. The entire team had a good year, but no single individual had a fantastic season.

Joe Morgan hit .327 and stole 67 bases. Pete hit .317 with 210 hits and a career-high 47 doubles. He also scored 112 runs. Johnny Bench hit 28 homers; George Foster, 23; and Tony Perez 20. Gary Nolan came back to win 15 games, as did Don Gullett and Jack Billingham. Freddie Norman, Clay Kirby, and rookie lefty Pat Darcy were also in double figures with wins.

The Pittsburgh Pirates overhauled the Philadelphia Phillies in the latter part of the season to win their fifth divisional title in six years. The Bucs had the second best record in the National League, but they were no match for the Reds in the Championship Series.

The Reds pounded out 12 hits and outscored the Pirates, 8-3, in Game One as Don Gullett went the distance and hit a homerun. They got another 12 hits in Game Two, and Tony Perez was the hitting star with 3 RBIs on a homer and a single. Pete got into the act in Game Three with a two-run shot in the eighth that gave the Reds a 3-2 lead, but the Pirates tied it in the ninth only to have Cincinnati score a pair in the tenth to win the game, 5-3, and series in a sweep.

It was World Series time, and the Reds prepared

themselves to face the Boston Red Sox. The Bean-towners had dethroned Oakland as American League champs by sweeping the A's in three games.

The Bosox had a very solid lineup that featured future Hall of Famer Carl Yastrzemski and AL Rookie-of-the-Year Fred Lynn and runner-up Jim Rice. Their starting rotation consisted of Bill Lee, Luis Tiant, Rick Wise, and Reggie Cleveland. Dick Drago, Diego Segui, and Jim Willoughby held up an adequate bullpen.

Game One was in Boston, and the Sox sent Luis Tiant to the mound against Gullett. Throwing a lefty at Fenway Park is considered to be suicidal, but Sparky Anderson had confidence in his ace. Gullett did the job for six innings, matching Tiant almost pitch for pitch as neither team could score. Then in the bottom of the seventh Boston broke it open with six runs and went on to win, 6-0.

Jack Billingham went up against Bill Lee in Game Two, and both pitchers were tough on their opponents. The Red Sox scored once in the first, and the Reds tied it in the fourth. Boston chased Billingham in the six with a run, but Pedro Borbon halted the rally, leaving the Reds behind, 2-1, until the ninth. Johnny Bench led off the last inning with a double. Boston manager Darrell Johnson pulled out Lee and brought in Drago who retired the first two men he faced. Then Davey Concepcion singled to score Bench. The diminutive short-stop from Venezuela then stole second and came racing home with the winning run on Ken Griffey's double. Rawley Eastwick held off Boston in the bottom half of the ninth, and the Series was tied at a game apiece.

The Series shifted to Cincinnati for Game Three, and it was just the beginning of the fireworks. Boston's catcher Carlton Fisk homered off Gary Nolan in the second to give the Red Sox an early 1-0 lead. Bench, Concepcion, and Geronimo each hit homers as the Reds mounted a 5-1 lead by scoring twice in the fourth and three times in the fifth. The Red Sox chipped away, scoring once each in the sixth and seventh, on run coming on a homer by former Reds' player Bernie Carbo. Then Bosox rightfielder Dwight Evans played his part in a World Series record by hitting the sixth homer of the game with a man on in the ninth to tie the game, 5-5. That set up the dramatic tenth inning. The Red Sox failed to score off Eastwick, and the Reds came to bat with Cesar Geronimo due to lead off. Geronimo singled, and Ed Armbrister tried to bunt him over to second. As Fisk tried to field the ball, he bumped into Armbrister who was heading for first base. Fisk made an errant throw to second that allowed both runners to advance a base, Geronimo to third and Armbrister to second. The Red Sox catcher claimed the Cincinnati outfielder interfered with him in an ensuing argument with the umpire, but everyone knows the umpire is always right. Joe Morgan singled later in the inning, and the Reds won, 6-5, to take a 2-1 lead in games.

In Game Four, the Red Sox used a five-run fourth inning to beat the Reds, 5-4, behind Tiant who threw 163 pitches while going the distance. The Series was now tied, but just getting exciting.

Tony Perez had been a bust so far in the Series, going

0-15 through the first four games, but in Game Five he came alive. With the Reds leading 2-1 in the bottom of the sixth, Perez belted a three-run blast to run the lead to four, then hit a solo shot in the eighth to put the game away for Cincinnati, 6-2.

Game Six was back in Boston. The Irish have a word for what this 12-inning affair turned out to be. They call it a donnybrook.

Freddie Lynn smacked a three-run homer in the bottom of the first to get the scoring started. The Reds tied it with a trio of tallies in the fifth, then took the lead with a pair in the seventh. A solo homer by Geronimo gave them a 6-3 lead in the eighth, but Carbo came up to pinchhit in the bottom of the frame with two on and he proceeded to slam his second homer of the Series to tie the game and set up the overtime play.

The Red Sox almost won it in the bottom of the ninth, but George Foster made a deadly throw home to nip Denny Doyle at the plate and squelch the rally. Dwight Evans returned the favor in the eleventh by making a leaping catch in rightfield to rob Joe Morgan of a homerun. In the bottom of the twelfth with Pat Darcy on the mound for Cincinnati, Fisk stepped to the plate for the Red Sox and boomed a cannon shot down the line to left. It was midnight on the East Coast, but all of America was up and awake and in front of the television amazed and delighted to see Fisk watch the ball as it flew toward the foul pole above the fence, his hands waving wildly as he danced in the direction of first base trying to coax the ball to stay fair. It did, striking the pole for a homer and giving the Red Sox an exciting 7-6 win to send the Series to seven games.

Game Seven was no less dramatic. Already, four games had been decided by one run, three of them in the final inning. Rain had delayed the final two games by washing out game days on the 18th, 19th, and 20th. A dozen homeruns had been hit already. And it all came down to one inning.

The Reds hadn't won a World Series title since 1940, but Boston hadn't had a champion since the 1918 Sox beat the Cubs 4 games to 2. The drought was coming to an end for one team but continuing for the other.

Both Gullett and Lee were well rested for the start of the last game. The Red Sox scored three times in the third, while Lee held the Reds in check over five. A two-run blast by Perez in the sixth narrowed the gap to 3-2, and Pete singled home a run in the seventh to tie it. That set up the ninth. The Reds put a man in scoring position with two outs and Joe Morgan coming to bat. The dynamite second sacker swung for the fences but only caught part of the ball, blooping a single to center to score the runner. Will McEnaney shut down the Red Sox in the home half of the inning, and the 1975 World Series was history. The Reds had won!

At last Pete had the championship ring he had coveted for so long. He thought he had earned about all the honors there were for a player to get, but more were in the offing. The sportswriters named him Most Valuable Player in the Series, and that got him a new car from Sport Magazine. Then Sports Illustrated gave him their Grecian urn for being their Sportsman of the Year. And finally the Hickok Company awarded

Pete the S. Rae Hickok Belt for Professional Athlete of the Year for 1975.

Upon receiving the diamond studded Hickok Belt, Pete remarked, "I'm not sure I deserved the last award I got here," referring to the SI award of Sportsman of the Year. "I am not a good sportsman. If I get my rear end kicked, I don't congratulate the guy who did it. I go to the dressing room and kick the door off my locker."

The Cincinnati Reds were kings of the Major League Baseball mountain when 1976 came around, and everyone was sure they were ready for a fall. They were cocky, arrogant, and obnoxious to those who didn't know them. But to those who did, the Reds were confident and positive, truly a professional team, epitomized by their unofficial leader, Pete Rose.

Howsam and Anderson knew a good thing when they saw it, and their team was a good one. The nucleus of the team had been same for seven years, and in that time they had won five divisional titles, three National League pennants, and at last the World Series. Now it was time to prove that the Reds of the 1970s deserved to be ranked among the all-time great teams in Baseball history.

Cincinnati only posted 102 wins in 1976, but they were enough to beat out the LA Dodgers by 10 full games for the NL West title. Seven Cincy pitchers won in double figures with Gary Nolan topping the list with 15 wins. Five regulars hit homers in double figures with George Foster coming into his own with 29 and Joe Morgan slamming 27. Johnny Bench had an off year with only 16 round-trippers and 74 RBIs, but his teammates picked up the slack.

Pete had a good year, too. He hit .323 with 215 hits, 42 doubles, 6 triples, 10 homers, 63 RBIs, and a career-high 130 runs scored. No MVP in '76 for Pete, but he felt the same as the sportswriters did when they chose Joe Morgan for the honor for the second straight year.

The Reds faced the Philadelphia Phillies in the Championship Series, and it was simply no contest. Cincy swept the Phils in three straight with Pete going 6-for-14 for a .429 average.

Over in the American League, Billy Martin was in his first term as skipper of the New York Yankees. Already he had managed the Minnesota Twins into the playoffs as well as the Detroit Tigers, and he had come close with the Texas Rangers. In 1975 after Martin was fired in Dallas, George Steinbrenner made the first smart move of his career as owner of the Yankees by snapping up Martin as soon as the firebrand manager was available. "Billy the Bully" screamed and shouted his Yanks to a first place finish in the AL East by 10½ games over the Orioles, then the Bronx Bombers won every other game against the Kansas City Royals in the League Championship Series, taking the final game on Chris Chambliss' lead-off homer in the bottom of the ninth of the fifth game to earn the right to face the Big Red Machine in the World Series.

The 1976 World Series! The New York Yankees! The Big Red Machine from Cincinnati the reigning champs. The Big Apple! All the elements for an exciting climax to a great baseball season that marked the 100th anniversary of professional baseball. It was more than fitting that the Cincinnati Reds, heirs to the very first professional baseball team, should be playing in the World Series.

If the 1976 Series had been a boxing match, the referee would have stopped the fight in the third round or in this case the third game. The Yankees were no where the equals of the Reds.

Game One went to the Reds on Tony Perez' three hits, Joe Morgan's homer, and some superb pitching by Don Gullett and Pedro Borbon. Reds 5, NY 1.

The second game was the only close one. It was tied going into the bottom of the ninth. The Yankee shortstop committed a costly error when his throw to first went into the dugout allowing Ken Griffey to reach second on the play. Perez promptly singled him home with the winning run. Reds 4, NY 3.

Game Three was all Reds. Dan Driessen had three hits, including a homer, and Pat Zachary and Will McEnaney held the Yanks to two runs on eight hits. Reds 6, NY 2.

Johnny Bench was the star of Game Four, cracking a pair of homers and knocking in five runs. He finished the Series with 8 hits in 15 trips for a .533 BA. Gary Nolan and McEnany earned the pitching honors, Nolan with the win and McEnany with the save. Reds 7, NY 2.

The Cincinnati Reds had reached the zenith of their history. There was no place higher to go.

16

Don't Go, Pete

When Pete signed with the Philadelphia Phillies, I wished him all the luck in the world. I know problems he had with the former management in Cincinnati, and I don't blame him for becoming a free agent.

In February 1979 Tony and I took a trip to Cincinnati to return the empty mailbags and give Pete things that came in the mail. We had planned on staying over at a motel, but Pete invited us to stay over at his home. Pete and Karolyn were always very hospitable, treating us like family and making us feel right at home.

The first thing Pete did when we sat down to chat was give Tony and I each a present. Tony received a beautiful wristwatch, and I received an electronic calculator and a small radio (to take to the ballgames with me). We still treasure them and intend to leave them to our grandchildren as mementoes of their grandparents and Pete Rose.

Pete and Karolyn had renovated their basement, and the walls were covered with trophies, pictures, and mementoes from his illustrious career. We picked up the mail that was there and went on to Riverfront Stadium to pick up the mail from the Reds. I'd thought we'd only get the mail from the end of the season to then, but Bernie Stowe, the equipment manager, gave us all the mail plus the contents of Pete's lockers and trunks which held items from earlier years. The trunk of our car, the back seat, and the floor were filled with boxes and bags of mail. The upstairs staff wanted Pete's things removed before spring training began, so everything that was his was added to the mail.

We tried very hard to get everything sorted and answered before Pete left for spring training. It was really a chore, but we made it.

Pete gave me his Phillies' pictures so that the outgoing mail would be up to date on the autographed photo, although some fans asked for a Cincinnati photo for their collections.

Many of the letters were from fans, wanting him to stay with the Reds. Many contained carbon copies of letters sent to the front office, blasting them for not giving Pete a decent contract or a raise to compensate all that he had done for the Reds.

One nice thing that the Cincinnati Reds officials did for Pete on his first trip back as a member of the Phillies was to retire number 14 in his honor.

Memo to Pete Rose,

I see by the papers that you are a free agent and that you would consider playing with the New York Yankees. Please spare us. We have enough Prima Donnas on the Yankees now, without having you on the team. You could never replace Reggie.

Perhaps the Mets might consider your application. Worth a try.

James

I had to smile when I read this one. This fellow was so right about the Yankees.

Dear Pete Rose,

My name is Mary ———. I am 12 years old and a Reds fan and a Pete Rose fan. It seems to me that money is more important to you than the Reds. So if you will remain on Cincinnati I will send you my life time savings of $492.32 wich I'm saving for college but to keep you on the Reds is more important

Love Always,

Mary

P.S. If you go to another team don't make it the Yankees. (I hate the Yankees).

Offering Pete her life savings was sweet, but he thought she would be better off to save it for something more worthwhile, like college. But what a gesture to make! It only shows how his fans feel about him.

Dear Pete:

You don't know me, I wish I could say we were the best of friends, but we're not. I first saw you when I was 9 years old at Crosley Field with my Dad, I'll never forget that day. You had walked, and sprinted to first base and my Dad pointed at you and said, "That's the way baseball should be played, 110% all the time, never cheat yourself". And I guess if there is only one reason why I have admired you all these years, its because you never quit, never gave less than all, you never cheated yourself. There's a lesson for those that want to see it, if all those people who have criticized you would look, they'll find that dedication ad determination pays off.

I don't feel betrayed by your leaving, it's something you had to do, and I admire you in some ways for having the guts to look elsewhere. It would have been easy to accept all the guff from Reds Management, and give in to them and sign, in order to stay in your home town but you wouldn't allow yourself to do that, you held your ground and made a decision that was I'm sure very tuff.

Your Friend,
Dave

Pete does have pride, and that was one reason for leaving Cincy. He is a great guy, and it isn't the fans who criticize Pete for doing what is best for him. True fans wish him the best, always.

Dear Pete Rose,

While my family was vacationing in Mexico, I bought a newspaper just for fun. Though I was not surprised, I looked through the sports section and found your picture and a story. I also saw you in the T.V. news down there.

All 5 of us are big fans of yours, and all the Cincinnati Reds.

Good Luck,
Mark

Doesn't it give you a wonderful feeling when you are in a strange land, you look through the newspaper and there's someone special that looks right back at you? I know the feeling! Pete Rose is a name that is known the world over.

Dear Pete,

You are my favorite baseball player. I have every baseball card of you since you were a rookie in 1963. I think your hitting streak was great and I have newspaper clippings since the 32nd game of your streak.

When my Dad was growing up his idol was Joe DiMaggio. My Dad was at the game when the Cleveland Indians stopped DiMaggio's streak and he told me nobody could ever break that record. I think you showed my Dad and the whole world that DiMaggio's record could be broken.

> *A great fan of yours,*
> *Tom*

I remember a song that was popular in the '40s. It was *Joltin' Joe DiMaggio*. And now we have *The Charlie Hustle* for Pete Rose. If you haven't heard it, you are missing something, believe me!

Dear Mr. Rose,

Recently, while visiting Clearwater, Florida during spring training I was shocked to hear the envious remarks that were made by the elderly people of America. What are your feelings toward the people who are envious of the money you make playing baseball? I feel that the constant pressure that you receive from people after and during the games is not some-

thing to be totally envious of. Is Billy Martin's constant struggle with society something to envy. Do we envy the millionaire that makes his money in insurance, politics, military weapons, oil or any other means. Its nice to know that a better man who takes his profession seriously can finally begin to adjust a slight tendency to overlook the individuals ability and not realize the importance of the individual concern for the welfare of his family.

The next time a reporter asks you about the monetary gains you have made in baseball, please relate these opinions to them.

I would appreciate it very much if you could answer some of the questions I would like answered by you.

1.) What are your honest feelings as to the owners pure interest in the game of baseball as a sport?

2.) What has the man Mr. Sparky Anderson done to increase your knowledge of the game?

3.) Would you ever decide to play for Japanese baseball in the future or what are your plans for the future?

I would like to thank you for the opportunity you have given me in the hope for people to achieve a goal in what profession they might enjoy.

Sincerely,
  Mr. Thomas

It's a sad commentary on America, a country that was built on free enterprise and the sweat of hard work, when people criticize a man or a woman for getting the most they can for their labor. It makes no difference whether that person is a baseball player or a factory worker. If someone is willing to pay more for the same job, why shouldn't you take it?

There are people who never try to get ahead in life, no dedication or hustle, and then wonder how they got passed by.

To answer this man's questions:

The owners are out to make a buck, and why shouldn't they be? They run the risks, they should make money. Does anyone feel sorry for an owner who loses his shirt on a sports franchise? Never! So why should anyone complain when he makes a few dollars? Some people say all employers should be willing to share the profits with the workers. But do they say the workers should share in the losses when the company goes broke? Not on your sweet life!

It would be hard to pinpoint exactly everything Pete learned from Sparky Anderson, but he did learn a lot.

Pete is very popular in Japan. He could probably make a lot of money over there, but money isn't everything to him.

As for his future, it's baseball. He'll play as long as he can contribute to the team, and when he can't do that any longer, he'll coach or manage.

Dear Pete Rose,

Do you remember about three years ago some girl threw you a daisy from the green section? You were in the left field at the time. Well, I'm that nut that threw you the daisy. I have a very important favor to ask of you.

You see, my mother likes you very much and I think you are the best player that has ever hit a baseball. Anyway my mother's fondest wish is to meet you one day.

My mother will be 52 August 22nd and we will be staying in the same hotel as the players. The favor I wish to ask you is— is there anyway you could come and meet my mother as a birthday gift from me? It will be a surprise for her. Also could you sign a baseball and give it to her. Pete, I would appreciate it very much because I can never think of what to get my mother for her birthday, and this is the ideal gift. Thank you very much Pete.

Joy

If Pete granted every request such as this, he wouldn't have time to play baseball. He had to pass this one up.

Dear Pete,
Thanks for starting The Pete Rose Fund. Its growth will mean a great deal to our baseball program here at UC. Best wishes to you and we'll look forward to seeing you when you return to Cincinnati.
Best wishes,
Bill

Pete doesn't keep all the money he makes.

Dear Mr. Rose:
I recently returned from a business and vacation trip to Belgium and while there had a most delightful experience that I must share with you.
During a stay of several days at Liege, Belgium, I was invited to talk with a group of Political Science students from the University. After an extensive introduction, which included

pointing out on a large map of the United States the exact location from which I came, I was asked my very first question. Of couse I expected to be quizzed about my reaction to President Carter, the Panama Canal, or the arms race. Much to my pleasure one of the young ladies verified that I was really from Cincinnati, Ohio, and then asked: "Did you see Mr. Rose hit his 3,000th hit?" My affirmative answer made me Hero No. 2, right after you.

After I returned home I got to thinking about this incident many times, and you can be sure that I think it is super that people like Pete Rose bring so much obvious pleasure to the world.

Very truly yours,
Tom

Dear Mr. Pete Rose:

I am writing you this letter to tell you some of the problems that I am having, and I am telling you the gods truth Mr. Rose. I don't know exactly how to say all of this, but I will try. My reason is as follows. The court ordered me to pay $50 a week for child support which I paid all along, until I lost my job. Becuase I got to the point as to where I didn't care about anything anymore after loosing my house, my kids, and my new car. I lost my job in January of '78, and I haven't found a good one since then.

I was getting so far behind in support I had to sell my other car I had in order to catch up the support that I was behind, and I'm still in the hole with a lot of other things also not only child support. Mr. Rose I need your help very badly, in order to get it all fixed up the way it should be. I have no way of getting around to good places for work because I have no car at all *now. And I would please like to know if you would please help me get another good car?*

I realize that you've gotten all types of letters, but all of this is the truth. Mr. Rose I am very sincere about this please believe me. Becuase I have no money at all and I am in an awful bad shape right now. I know you personally from meeting you at the stadium in Cincinnati when I tried out for the Reds farm club. I am a tremendous fan of yours, and I allways will be.

So please Mr. Rose help me in some way, I would deeply appreciate it very very much.

Mick

This poor fellow is under the impression that Pete is a loan company or a bank or a philanthropist. The sad thing is he isn't alone. Pete must get a hundred letters like this one a week, all of them very sincere and very demanding. And they aren't all from individuals. In some form or another, everyone of them is asking for a handout instead of a hand up.

Pete is well off financially, no doubt about that. But he works for his money and believes everyone should do the same thing. Hustling isn't limited to the athletic field. It applies to every walk of life. Pete's dad worked in a bank, but he still hustled at it. You get paid to produce, not sit around and talk about it.

Pete produces. Just check his records.

17

Good-bye, Cincy

Loyalty is a two-way street. You give and you should get equal treatment in return. In 1978 Pete tired of giving and not getting.

For 16 seasons Pete had played baseball for the Cincinnati Reds, and every year he gave them 110%. But the Reds' management failed to reward Pete according to his production on the field. Instead they fought with Pete and/or his agent every winter over money, never paying Pete what he was worth to the team, never paying him a salary that put him on a level with other stars of the game.

Pete wanted to be the first singles hitter to get a contract worth $100,000. He succeeded in that. But the homerun hitters were getting $200,000 then. So Pete set his sights higher and got bigger contracts, but as his salary escalated the power boys got paid more and more. Even some pitchers were getting more.

Then Catfish Hunter got out of his contract with Oakland, and the free-agency era began. The Dodgers'

Andy Messersmith and Montreal's Dave McNally then went to arbitration, and they were released from their contracts. The reserve clause that Curt Flood had tried to break in court five years before was finally being dealt with effectively.

Major League owners tried a lock-out of players at training camp in the spring of 1976, refusing to let the players practice without a contract between the Players Association and the owners. Commissioner Bowie Kuhn got the players to soften their stance on the reserve clause and ordered the owners to open the camps on March 17.

Later that year an agreement was reached whereby the reserve clause was retained but not with the same force it had known for decades. No longer would a player be bound to one team until his contract was traded or sold or the team released him from it. A five-year veteran could demand to be traded and would have the right to veto the first six teams he was offered to. If he was not traded, he could become a free agent. A player with six years in the Majors could play out his contract and become a free agent, throwing his name into a pool from which all the Major League teams could draft players. Each player could be drafted by 12 teams as well as his original team. The player could then negotiate with those 13 teams.

The first free agent draft was held in November 1976, and only 24 players were in it. Three of those players were not drafted by anyone, but those that were became some of the highest paid talent in sports. In addition to that select group were players who had one year left on their contracts and would be eligible for free agency at the end of the 1977 season. The Dodgers Don Sutton was among these men. In order to keep their ace, Los Angeles gave Sutton, who had made $155,000 in 1976, a four-year contract worth $1 million.

More millionaires were made in 1977 with the second free agent draft. Some of these *nouveau riche* baseball players had a lot less talent or fewer credentials than Pete had. He asked the Reds to put his bank account in the same class as his production on the field, but the Cincinnati management held firm. So Pete opted to play out his contract in 1978.

The bidding for Pete's services was hot and furious. He was drafted by the maximum number of teams, and almost every one them offered him $1 million or more. The Atlanta Braves made the sweetest offer of all — a cool million bucks per season and $100,000 a year more for the rest of his life. The Pirates, Cardinals, and Kansas City Royals each made substantial proposals, all higher than the Philadelphia Phillies.

But money isn't everything, especially to Pete. He wanted more than money. He wanted to play baseball. None of the other teams offered Pete any guarantees concerning his playing time. Pete also likes to win, and he didn't want to play for a team that didn't have excellent potential for making the playoffs and the World Series. The latter fact eliminated the Braves and Cards, both finishing 69-93 in '78. The Pirates had finished 1½ games behind Philadelphia, the NL East Division winner that year. The Royals had won their division in the American League for the third consecutive year. Of the three winners, Philadelphia guaranteed Pete a chance to break Stan Musial's National League record of 3,630 hits. He already had 3,164 hits, and being only 37 years old Pete felt he still had at least five more good years left to play. The Phillies offered Pete a four-year deal worth $3 million, making him the highest paid player in the game at the time. With an option year added on, Pete would have the five years of playing time he wanted.

But maybe money wasn't the only reason Pete took the free agency route. Maybe he felt he was no longer wanted by the Reds' management. They couldn't trade Pete, not without his permission because he had been with the Reds for over 15 years. So just maybe he wanted to find out who really desired his services. Or maybe he was angry with the front office for two of the dumbest moves ever made in the history of Baseball.

Ten days before Christmas 1976 the Reds gave Tony Perez an unusual gift; they traded him to the Montreal Expos along with Will McEnaney for pitchers Woodie Fryman and Dale Murray. Tony was all of 34 at the time, and his statistics seemed to be on decline. The immortal Branch Rickey had once said that it was best to trade a player after a great year when his value was still high. Perez hadn't had a great year in 1976, but there was still some zing in his swing, enough for Montreal but not enough for Cincinnati.

The Reds had won two straight World Series with Perez. In 1977, they finished second, 10 games behind the Dodgers and with the only the fourth best record in the National League. Numberswise, many of the Reds had fantastic seasons. George Foster hit a Major League high of 52 homers with 49 RBIs and a BA of .320. Johnny Bench rebounded with 31 homeruns and 109 RBIs. Dan Driessen hit 17 homers with 91 RBIs and a BA of .300. Pete had his ninth season of over 200 hits, reaching safely 204 times, and he had his twelfth year with a BA over .300, hitting .311.

After a few minor trades in the off season, the Reds were still pretty much the same team in 1978 as they had been in 1976. The pitching staff was changed considerably with only Pedro Borbon and Freddie Norman remaining, but the every day lineup with the exception of Perez was identical. Still, the Reds finished second again, this time only 2½ games behind Los Angeles. Foster had another big year with 40 homers and 120 RBIs. Pete barely missed 200 hits, getting 198 and averaging .302 for the year. The pitching just wasn't there to win a title.

The biggest news of all in '78 was Pete. On Opening Day he played in his 653rd consecutive game, breaking the Cincinnati club record set by Frank McCormick. On May 5 he became the 13th player in the history of Major League Baseball to get 3,000 hits when he singled off Montreal's Steve Rogers.

But the biggest news of all started quietly on June 14. Pete got a hit off Chicago's Dave Roberts. It wasn't all that important then. It was later because Pete got a hit in his next game and the one after that and the one after that and so on until he had at least one hit in 44 consecutive games. On July 25 he broke Tommy Holmes post-1900 National League record of 37 straight games when he singled off New York's Craig Swan, and on July 31 he tied Wee Willie Keeler's all-time National League record of 44 straight set in 1897 when he rapped out a safety off Phil Niekro of Atlanta. In Game 45, Larry McWilliams and Gene Garber of the Braves halted his string, and Joe DiMaggio's all-time record of 56 games was still safe.

Pete complained after the game that Garber had pitched "like it was the seventh game of the World Series." Pete later regretted the remarks, but at the time they were understandable. Atlanta was beating the Reds, 16-4, and it was the ninth inning.

Garber remarked in pure Pete Rose style: "I have an idea that if I was pitching like it was the seventh game of the World Series, he was hitting like it was the ninth inning of the seventh game of the World Series. I wanted his streak to continue, but I wanted to get him out, too. That's what I get paid to do."

Pete can't argue with that.

It was easy to shrug off the trade of Pete's long-time friend Tony Perez, but when the Reds' front office made the second dumb move, Pete started looking for the handwriting on the wall. Sparky Anderson was fired after the 1978 season.

How can a team fire a manager who led them to three second place finishes, five divisional titles, three pennants, and two world titles in nine seasons? Did the Dodgers fire Walt Alston after the 1958 season when the Bums finished seventh in an eight-team league? No. Why? Because Alston had led the Dodgers to two pennants and a World Series victory only three years before. He went on to win the pennant and the World Series in 1959, 1963, and 1965, adding pennants in 1966 and 1974. The Dodgers' management knew the secret to success is continuity. All the great teams in history have that one common denominator. Even the Reds had it in the 70s.

So just maybe Pete left Cincinnati because he was upset over the trade of Perez and the firing of Sparky Anderson. Those two moves may not be the entire reason, but they did contribute to his decision.

The signing of Pete Rose by the Phillies was compared to another great autograph day in Philadelphia history. Some sportswriters said it ranked right up there with John Hancock putting his signature on the Declaration of Independence in 1776.

During an interview in spring training, Pete said, "I'm happy to be a Phillie. I think I can help them get in the World Series."

So did everyone else.

The Philadelphia Phillies spent a decade recovering from their infamous collapse of 1964. The front office had worked very hard to put together a solid contender by the middle of the 1970s. They started in 1972 by trading righthander Rick Wise to the Cardinals for lefty Steve Carlton who was so happy to get out of St. Louis that he went 27-10 in '72 for a Philadelphia team that won only 59 games for the whole season. Philadelphia had a scrappy switchhitting shortstop named Larry Bowa from out of their farm system. Two sluggers, outfielder Greg Luzinski and thirdbaseman Mike Schmidt, as well as catcher Bob Boone, came up through the organization. They traded for outfielders Bake McBride and Garry Maddox, secondbaseman Manny Trillo, catcher Tim McCarver, and pitchers Jim Lonborg, Tug McGraw, and Jim Kaat.

They added a little more home-grown talent and by 1976 the Phillies were winners of the NL East. They won the division in '77 and again '78, but each year they lost the playoffs, first to Pete and the Big Red Machine of Cincinnati, then twice in a row to the Los Angeles Dodgers. Each time they lost in post-season play it seemed all they needed was one more key hit to make them winners. The Phillies were hoping that the addition of Pete would give them that player who could get them those key hits.

Although Pete had an outstanding year in 1979, the rest of the Phillies couldn't come up with matching seasons. Pete hit .331 in 163 games, finishing second to Keith Hernandez of the Cardinals who hit .344. He was third best in hits with 208 behind St. Louis shortstop Gary Templeton, 211, and Hernandez, 210. It was the tenth time he had gotten more than 200 safeties in a season, breaking Ty Cobb's career mark of nine 200-plus hits seasons. He was elected to the NL All-Star team for the 13th time in 17 years, becoming the first player ever elected at four different positions.

Philadelphia finished a distant fourth, 14 games behind Pittsburgh. The Pirates had put on a late rush to snatch the title away from the Montreal Expos on the last weekend of the season.

Once more Pete sat in front of his television and watched the playoffs and World Series. The hard part of it was seeing the Reds, winners of the NL West by 1½ games over Houston, lose to the Pirates. Baltimore disposed of California handily, and the Pirates and Orioles were set for a rematch of their 1971 Octoberfest.

Earl Weaver and the weather helped the Birds get off to a good start as Baltimore won the opener, 5-4. Pittsburgh won the second game, but the O's came back to win the next two. Down 3 games to 1 the Pirates faced a hill very few had climbed before them. But they did it, sweeping the final three games to win the Series. Willie Stargell was voted the MVP of the Series, and the song *We Are Family* came to be identified with the Pirates.

One more time Pete had to "wait 'til next year."

Next year came and the Phillies were ready.

Dallas Green took over as manager of the Phillies with 30 games to go in the 1979 season. He won 19 of them, but it wasn't enough to overhaul Pittsburgh. Green was Pete's kind of manager: tough but fair. And he was a winner, a man who would settle for nothing less than all-out effort. Pete was his kind of player.

Philadelphia almost didn't make it to the playoffs in 1980. Montreal had a very strong team and an excellent manager in Dick Williams who was in his fourth year at the helm. Williams had won pennants in Boston ('67) and Oakland ('72-'73). He had brought the Expos close in '79 as they finished only 3 games behind Pittsburgh. He came closer in 1980 losing out to the Phillies by only one game.

With the exceptions of Mike Schmidt (40 HRs and 121 RBIs) and Bake McBride (.309 and 87 RBIs), none of the Phildadelphia regulars had outstanding years. Not even Pete. He hit .282 with only 185 hits. Steve Carlton was fantastic on the mound winning 24 games, and Dick Ruthven won 17. Tug McGraw saved 20 games, mostly in the latter part of the season. The part-time play of Lonnie Smith in left field didn't hurt as he hit .339 and gave the Phils speed on the basepaths.

The biggest factor to the Phillies' success was they were a team of gamers. When they needed that key hit to win, they got it. When they went into a short losing streak, they had a stopper in Carlton, and when he was off, Ruthven took up the slack. This fact became evident first in the Championship Series, then the World Series.

Houston played catch-up baseball all year long, using speed, defense, and superb pitching to catch the Dodgers and force them into a one-game playoff for the NL West title. Joe Niekro, who had been the best pitcher in the Majors during the second half of the year, beat LA to give the Astros their first ever title.

A two-run homer by Greg Luzinski gave the Phils and Carlton the nod in Game One. The Astros rebounded in Game Two, winning, 7-4, in 10 innings with a four-run outburst in the top of the tenth. Niekro came on to pitch 10 scoreless innings in Game Three but wasn't the winning pitcher when Joe Morgan tripled to lead off the bottom of the eleventh inning before scoring on Denny Walling's sacrifice fly off Tug McGraw. The Phillies overcame a 2-0 deficit by scoring three runs in the eighth in Game Four, but the Astros tied it in the ninth to send the game into extra innings. Pete singled and scored the winning run as Philadelphia pushed a pair of tallies across in the tenth to tie the series at 2 games each.

Game Five was the most exciting Championship Series game played to that time. Houston scored once in the bottom of the first. The Phillies came back with a pair in the second. A single run in the bottom of the sixth tied it for the Astros, then they went ahead with three runs in the bottom of the seventh to make the score 5-2. Then the Phillies got cooking off "The Express" Nolan Ryan. They rallied for five runs in the eighth to go up, 7-5. The Astros retaliated with a pair in their half of the inning to tie the game at 7-all. Neither team could score in the ninth, and the series saw its fourth straight overtime game, a record. Garry Maddox doubled home Del Unser in the top of the tenth, and Ruthven held the Astros scoreless in the bottom of the frame to make the Phillies National League champs for the first time since 1950.

Pete had a great series, getting 8 hits in 20 official trips with 5 walks and 3 runs scored.

The Kansas City Royals won the American League West three years in a row from 1976-78, the same as the Phillies had done in the National League East. And three straight times the Royals were beaten in the Championship Series by the New York Yankees. Just like the Phillies, things were different in 1980. The Royals swept the Yankees in three games.

The Royals had won their division handily by 14 games, primarily on the strength of thirdbaseman George Brett's bat and the arm of submarining relief pitcher Dan Quisenberry. Brett came within an eyelash of becoming the first .400 hitter since Ted Williams hit .406 in 1941. He finished with a .390 average, 24 homers, and 118 RBIs, which is only incredible since he only played 110 games. Quisenberry had 33 saves and 12 wins coming out of the bullpen 75 times to stop the opposition.

Dallas Green and Jim Frey of Kansas City were both rookie managers. Frey had tutored under Baltimore's Earl Weaver, but unlike Weaver who believed power and pitching were all you needed to win, Frey was a proponent of speed. And the Royals had plenty, having led the AL with 185 stolen bases that year. Green was more like Weaver. He went for power and pitching.

The two teams appeared to be evenly matched going into Game One. Willie Mays Aikens hit a two-run shot in the second inning to give Kansas City a 2-0 lead, and Amos Otis made the score 4-0 with two-run blast in the third. The Phillies got a three-run slam out of Bake McBride in the bottom of the inning as they scored five times to take the lead, 5-4. Single tallies in the fourth and fifth innings gave the Phils a 7-4 lead going into the eighth when Aikens pounded out another two-run homer. Tug McGraw got the final six outs, and the Phils won their first World Series game since 1915 and their second of all time.

They didn't have to wait that long to win their third October Classic contest. A four-run rally in the bottom of the eighth inning off Quisenberry carried Philadelphia to a 6-4 win in Game Two.

Quisenberry redeemed himself in Game Three as the

Series shifted to Kansas City. The ace reliever put down a Philadelphia rally in the top of the eighth that tied the game and sent it into extra innings, then held the Phils scoreless the rest of the way. Aikens tripled in the bottom of the tenth to score Willie Wilson from first base to give the Royals their first ever World Series victory, 4-3.

Game Four went to the Royals also. Aikens became the first player ever to have two multiple homerun games in the same Series when he belted a two-run shot in the first inning and a solo homer in the second as the Royals won, 5-3.

The Phillies staged a ninth-inning rally off Quisenberry in Game Five as Del Unser doubled home Mike Schmidt, then scored on a single by Manny Trillo. Tug McGraw shut out the Royals for the third inning in a row in the ninth, and the Phillies headed home with their third win, 4-3.

Steve Carlton was called upon to wrap up the title for the Phillies in Game Six. He responded by throwing seven shutout innings, leaving the game with a 4-0 lead. McGraw came on to finish the job but gave up a solo run in the eighth and allowed the Royals to load the bases with one out in the ninth. With the game on the line, Frank White of Kansas City popped up in foul territory. Phillie catcher Bob Boone had a play on it. The ball hit his mitt and popped out, but the greatest gamer of them all, Pete Rose, was on the job doing his duty. Pete snatched the ball out of the air, and White was out. McGraw got the next man, and the Phillies won the Series.

Two years of Pete's contract with the Phillies had been fulfilled. Pete was living up to his end of the bargain; the Phillies were winners and World Champs. And the Philadelphia management was living up to its end; Pete was playing every day.

There was a reasonable explanation for Pete's stats to decline for the 1974 season, the aforementioned off-field distraction of writing a book on that campaign. Another off-field problem came along in 1979 to interfere with Pete's concentration on the playing field.

Actually, it was a problem and it wasn't. On the positive side, Pete had met a new lady and had fallen in love. On the negative side, the press was making hay with his personal life, portraying him as a playboy type who was running around behind his wife's back, some stories intimating that he had two or three girls in every National League city and one in every AL city. Pete denied this in an interview with *Sports Illustrated.*

"Not a *lot* of ladies," he said. "It was always just one at a time."

Jimmy Piersall tattled on Major Leaguers in his most recent book, writing that ballplayers chased as many skirts as they did flyballs and a lot of them banged out more homers off the field than on. He also wrote that most Major League wives tolerate this situation because their husbands bring home such good money.

Whether Piersall's evaluation of Major League life off the field applies to Pete or not is Pete's business, the same as any other private citizen. But the media is apt to degrade itself by reporting such things in print or on the tube. They argue that the public wants to know these things, and from looking at the enormous sales of so many scandal sheets, they may be correct in that assumption. The question still remains: Why do legitimate family newspapers print the dirt about public figures? In the case of athletes, some psychologists have written that many sportswriters are frustrated jocks, green with envy over the success and prowess of professionals and that they try to bring these superior people down to their size by writing scandalous stories about their personal lives. The same has been applied to film critics and art reviewers. George Bernard Shaw once said, "Those who can, do; those who cannot, teach." A famous actor once paraphrased Shaw, saying, "Those who can, act; those who cannot, criticize."

As for Pete, the facts are that he was married and had two children when he met Carol Woilung. She didn't even know who he was at the time, but it made no difference to her. She liked him for the person he is, not for him being the famous "Charlie Hustle". Because Pete is not one to enter into sordid relationships, he dated Carol openly. His wife Karolyn couldn't tolerate a situation such as that and sued for divorce.

A divorce means a change in one's life, a big change that is not always pleasant. Pete went through the divorce, and it affected him the same as it would any man or woman. Although he and Carol were married, the hard part for him was not seeing his children as often as he had before. That all changed later on when Tyler Edward Rose was born.

As the 1981 season rolled around, Pete's off-field problems were behind him, but one on-field faced him.

Major League Baseball had had its problems in the past, and almost all of them concerned the relationship between the players and the owners. The players had gone out on strike at the beginning of the 1972 season, and they were threatening to do it again in 1981. The question was when and for how long. In '72, the strike had lasted only a few weeks, hardly affecting the schedule. That was not the plan in '81.

Pete had signed with Philadelphia because they promised to let him play so he could pursue Stan Musial's National League record for hits in a career. Pete was only 73 hits away from that record when the season started. Could he catch Musial before the strike came or not? The strike was set for the last out of the last game to be played on June 11. The Phils had 55 games scheduled to that date. Pete would have to get 1.345 hits per game to break Musial's record before the strike. Considering he had averaged 1.257 hits per game in his career prior to 1981, this was a tall order.

Also in the back of Pete's mind were other figures. Musial's NL record for doubles in a career, 725; Hank Aaron's career hit total of 3,771; Aaron's Major League record for games played in a career, 3,298; Aaron's Major League record for times at bat in a career, 12,364; Aaron's NL record for runs scored in a career, 2,107; Ty Cobb's Major League record for runs scored in a career, 2,245; and finally, the granddaddy of all lifetime batting records, Cobb's Major League record for hits in a career, 4,191.

But first things first; climb one hill at a time; and the first one was Musial's hit record.

The Phillies opened the season with pretty much the same cast as that which had led them to World Series title the year before. The only exception was Greg Luzinski was gone from leftfield, replaced by Gary Matthews who had signed on as a free agent. Philadelphia picked up where they had left off by pounding their opponents into submission. Pete picked up where he had left off the 1979 season. As the strike approached, the Phillies had a firm hold on first place and Pete was hitting over .300. The Phils last game before the strike was set for June 10 against the Houston Astros in Philadelphia. As that date drew nearer, so did Pete to Musial's record.

Finally, the stage was set. Pete had 72 hits for the year, 3,629 for his career. Nolan Ryan, "The Express", was on the mound for Houston. A crowd of 57,386 that included "Stan the Man" himself was on hand at Veterans Memorial Stadium.

Pete came to bat in the bottom of the first. Ryan delivered the ball. Pete swung. The ball looped toward the outfield. It fell safely. Pete raced around first, held up, and went back to first amid the standing ovation from the crowd. He tipped his hat in acknowledgement. The game went on.

Bottom of the third, Ryan was on a roll. He wasn't about to let Pete break any records if he could stop him. Strike one! Strike two! Strike three! The record would have to wait another trip to the plate.

Last of the fifth, Pete was bearing down. So was Ryan. Pete ran the count to 2-2. Ryan came in with a curve. Pete expected a fastball. Strike three! No record yet. And from the way Ryan was pitching, it appeared Pete would only get one more shot at it before the strike deadline.

This was it. Home half of the eighth. Pete was due up. Ryan rared back and fired. Strike one! Again, strike two! A slider for a ball. The count was 1-2. In came the express. Pete swung. The crowd held its collective breath. Nothing but air. Strike three! Pete Rose and Stan Musial would share the record until the strike was over, whenever that would be.

The Major League owners finally ran out of insurance money in early August, and Commissioner Bowie Kuhn finally did his job and got both sides to agree on something so the season could resume. There would be no making up the games that were cancelled by the strike. The season would be divided into two halves. Each of the four division leaders at the time of the strike would go into a playoff for the division title whereby the winners of the first half would square off against the winners of the second half and the two survivors would then meet to determine the pennant winner. It was the only way to get the fans, most of whom were terribly upset with both the owners and the players, back into the stadia.

It was two months to the day. Same playing field; bigger crowd of 60,561, including Musial again; the St. Louis Cardinals were the opponent. Pete was 0-for-3 when he came up in the bottom of the eighth. Mark Littell was on the mound for the Cards. In came the pitch. Pete swung. A roller toward left. It had eyes as it slipped between Templeton and Oberkfell for a hit.

Pete Rose had the record and had surpassed one of the Game's immortals, thus immortalizing himself.

With that excitement behind him, Pete settled down to the rest of the season. He wound up hitting .325, second to Pittsburgh's Bill Madlock at .341. He led the league in hits for the seventh time, a National League record. He finished second in runs scored with 73.

The Phillies were in the playoffs by virtue of their 34-21 record in the first half. Montreal won the second half. Los Angeles won the first half in the West, and Houston won the second half. In the American League, the New York Yankees won the East first half and the Milwaukee won the second half; Oakland won the West first half and Kansas City the second half.

Steve Rogers and Bill Gullickson started and won the first two games of the playoffs for Montreal with relief help from Jeff Reardon in both contests. The series switched to Philadelphia for Game Three, and the Phils rapped out 13 hits, Gary Matthews getting three, in support of Larry Christenson to win, 6-2. The Phillies won the fourth game in 10 innings, 6-5, on a pinchhit homer by George Vukovich. Steve Rogers was back on the mound for the deciding game, opposed by Steve Carlton. Rogers had the better game, shutting out the Phils, 3-0, and putting the Expos into a playoff with the Dodgers for the pennant.

The Dodgers had come from behind, down 2-0 in games, to defeat the Astros, then came from behind again against the Expos, winning in five games by taking the last two in Montreal.

The Yankees took the Brewers in five, then swept the

Royals who had done likewise to Oakland. Another Fall Classic was at hand.

The first two games were in New York, and the Yankees won them in unspectacular fashion. Out in Los Angeles the Dodgers won three straight, each by one run. In New York for Game Six, the Dodger hitters finally poured it on and smashed the Yankees, 9-2, to win the Series, 4 games to 2. Afterward, Yankee owner George Steinbrenner apologized to the people of New York for his team's embarrassing failure to beat the Bums from the West Coast. The sportswriters had fun with that one.

Pete had nothing to apologize for at the end of the year. If he had retired at that point, satisfied with only having broken Musial's record, he would have hung up his spikes with 3,697 hits in 11,910 trips to the plate for a career batting average of .310. He would also have had 1,915 runs scored, 672 doubles, and 2,937 games played. He was 75 hits short of passing Hank Aaron for the number two spot on the all-time list; 54 doubles short Musial's NL record; 140 games short of Aaron's NL record; already had the record for most times at-bat in the National League and was 454 trips short of Aaron's Major League record; 193 runs short of Aaron's NL record; and 495 hits short of Cobb's Major League record of 4,191 hits.

But Pete had one year and an option year left on his contract with the Phillies. That meant two full seasons in which he could break some of those records.

Dallas Green stepped down as the manager of the Phillies and accepted the post of general manager of the

Chicago Cubs. Pat Corrales took the reins in Philadelphia. Age was beginning to show on the Phillies. Pete was 40; Larry Bowa, 36; Bob Boone, 34; Garry Maddox, 32; Bake McBride, 32; Mike Schmidt, 32; Manny Trillo, 31; Gary Matthews, 31; Steve Carlton, 37; Ron Reed, 39; and Tug McGraw, 37. New GM Paul Owens felt the Phillies needed some new blood, and Dallas Green was willing to help him out.

The first to go was Lonnie Smith, to St. Louis by way of Cleveland in three-way deal for catcher Bo Diaz. Owens then sold Boone to California. Keith Moreland, Dan Larsen, and Dickie Noles were next, to the Cubs for Mike Krukow and cash. Owens and Green coveted the other's shortstop, so Bowa went to the Cubs for Ivan DeJesus. Owens wanted DeJesus so badly that he threw in Ryne Sandberg as part of the deal. Little did Owens know that Green wanted Sandberg more than he wanted Bowa. The last to go was McBride who went to Cleveland for Sid Monge.

The Phillies had a new look for 1982, and it affected their play. Trillo and DeJesus had been teammates in Chicago for two years in 1977-78, and they made a better doubleplay combination than Bowa and Trillo had. Diaz was a better all-around catcher than Boone in all but one respect: Boone was smarter and called a better game. For all practical purposes, the Phillies were a better team.

The only thing was Lonnie Smith and Willie McGee in St. Louis' outfield and Ozzie Smith at short made the Cardinals the best team in the National League. Philadelphia finished second in the East. Atlanta won the

West, then proved lefthanded pitching is a must if a team wants to win the pennant as Whitey Herzog's Cardinals swept the Braves. The Cardinals proved their point by beating the Milwaukee Brewers in the World Series, winning four of the five games started by Milwaukee righties and losing both games started by lefty Mike Caldwell. Milwaukee's two lefthanded pitchers allowed 10 earned run in 23 innings for an ERA of 3.91, while their righthanders allowed 22 earned runs in 37 innings for an ERA of 5.35.

Pete had a down year. His numbers were proof of it. His average tumbled .054 to .271. His hits dropped from 1.308 per game to 1.062 per game. People were beginning to say that he was on his way out and that the only thing that was keeping him in the Game was his guaranteed contract. Some were saying he should quit before he began embarrassing himself and his team.

Anyone who knows Pete knows Pete is not a quitter. He will never give up on himself or his team. He will do whatever it takes to win. That means hustling, and that's all Pete Rose knows.

At the end of the 1982 season, Pete signed a one-year contract with the Phillies that included a buy-out clause whereby they would have to pay Pete $300,000 if they decided not to renew that contract by November 15, 1983. The Phillies felt Pete would bounce back from his off year in '82.

Going into the 1983 season, Pete had 3,869 hits, having passed Hank Aaron on June 22, 1982 with a double off John Stuper of the Cardinals at Busch Stadium. He had 1,995 runs scored, 697 doubles, 3,099

Dear Pete   **241**

games played, 12,544 times at-bat, and a career batting average of .308. If all he did was duplicate the year before, he would pass the 4,000-hit mark and be within one-season striking distance of Cobb's mark of 4,191.

But it wasn't to be. Pete struggled in 1983. He played every day under Pat Corrales, then Paul Owens came down from the front office when Corrales was fired after 85 games and a record of 43-42. Owens kicked the Phillies into high gear, partly by replacing Pete with his old friend Tony Perez at first and platooning Perez with rookie Len Matuszek during the month of September. Pete was used as a pinchhitter, and he responded by getting 8 hits in 22 trips for a .373 average. The move worked because Matuszek and Perez contributed a great deal down the stretch, and the Phils won the NL East going away by 6 games over the Pirates.

The Dodgers won the West, but the Phillies polished them off in four games to win the pennant. Pete played all four games at first base and had 6 hits in 16 trips, scoring 3 runs. Matuszek was ineligible for the playoffs and World Series, not having been recalled from the minors until September 1.

Baltimore beat the Chicago White Sox in four games to reach the Series. It looked like a good match. The O's had more power and solid hitting. The Phils had more speed, pitching, and defense. It turned out to be a dull affair. Philadelphia won the opener, but Baltimore came back with a vengeance to take the next four.

Pete was in a quandary with the end of the baseball season. The Phillies intended to have Paul Owens manage the team again in 1984, and that meant Pete would be platooned at first and used as a pinchhitter. Because Matuszek, his intended replacement, was a lefthanded hitter, Pete would be starting less than 50 games and maybe get into another 50 as a pinchhitter or substitute for Matuszek. This would mean he would only get to bat 250 times or so. He would have to hit .400 to get 100 hits, and that wasn't likely. This was intolerable situation for Pete.

There was only one thing to do.

18

A Special Letter

There is only one letter in this chapter. It isn't written to Pete, but a copy of it was sent to him by its author. I felt it deserved special attention, and I think you will agree after you read it.

The addressee, Lewis Grizzard, was a writer for the Atlanta *Constitution* newspaper at the time which was right after Pete had his 44-game hitting streak stopped by the Braves' Larry McWilliams and Gene Garber.

Dear Mr. Grizzard:

I have always enjoyed reading your column in the paper, ever since your first article on returning from Chicago. Having originally been from the "Windy City", I could appreciate your views, and found your observations of my home town very entertaining.

Your article last week on Pete Rose was one which I would like to take issue with, and disagree with you for the first time. The terminology you used to end your article, and last description of Pete was "BUSH". I don't think you know Pete and could be fair in your analysis of this man. I would like to show the other side of a beautiful person. There are very few professional athletes who would take the time and have the patience to deal with the public as this man has. Phil Niekro is the other exception of this rare breed.

I have a fifteen year old son who loves sports, has participated in all sports activities, and has been excit-ing to all who have watched him. His one handicap is that he stand 4'9" and is known to all of his friends and "Peanuts". Although his size might be a handicap to others, he plays high school basketball, Sandy Koufax baseball, and plays a very competitive game of tennis. Where does a child this size get the inspiration to even participate? Ten years ago "Peanuts" adopted Pete Rose as his idol. He has patterned himself after this man. Three years ago on his 12th birthday, I had a party at the stadium prior to a Braves-Reds game. The day before the game I called the Marriott Hotel and asked to speak to Pete Rose. To my amazement, I was connected with him. I explained to Pete how this young man admired and respected him. He invited Peanuts and me to come down to the hotel the day of the game and have lunch with him. Pete spent the whole afternoon with this young man, took him to the game on the team bus, spent the pre-game in the locker room with him, and then took him out on the field and played pepper with him. He then proceeded to give Peanuts his bat. Pete's parting words to Peanuts were to do well in school, as this was his biggest personal mistake in life. Peanuts has been an A-B student since this big day three years ago. Pete's influence has been a major factor on a boy who is small in size but big on desire. I am proud that this boy is my son, and hope you don't mind me taking issue with your description of the man who has inspired my boy, and many

more of our youth today. If we had more baseball players with
this winning attitude, baseball would probably be better off.
  Cordially,
  Ronnie

If Baseball had a Mt. Rushmore, don't you think one
of the four faces carved in it would have to belong to
Pete Rose? Of course, I'm prejudiced because of my
personal proximity to Pete. But the letters in this book
are only a sample of the hundreds of thousands he has
received over the years, and they support my feelings
about him.

How many mothers and fathers want their sons and
daughters to be like Pete Rose? How many parents
want their children to try to be the best they can be?

19

The Big Knock

The time: *7:59 P.M. EDT.*
The date: *September 11, 1985.*
The place: *Riverfront Stadium, Cincinnati, Ohio.*

On a warm afternoon exactly 57 years earlier, Tyrus Raymond Cobb went to bat for the last time as a Major League Baseball player. Eight days earlier he had collected his last hit, a double off Washington pitcher Bump Hadley. It was the 4,191st of his 24-year career that had begun in 1905 when he was called up from the minors to play the outfield for the Detroit Tigers. When he retired at the end of the 1928 season, people said he had established records that would never be broken.

They were wrong.

First Babe Ruth broke Cobb's career record for most extra base hits. Cobb had 1,139, and Ruth finished with 1,356. Lou Gehrig then passed Cobb in the lifetime standings with 1,190. Stan Musial passed all three and set a new high with 1,377. Willie Mays passed Gehrig and Cobb before retiring with 1,323. Hank Aaron then topped them all with 1,477. After Aaron did it, Frank Robinson and Carl Yastrzemski also passed Cobb.

Stan Musial broke Cobb's career record for total bases by totaling 6,134 to Cobb's 5,863. Mays also surpassed Cobb, but Aaron topped them all by getting 6,856 in his illustrious career.

Aaron beat Cobb's record of 11,429 times at-bat with 12,364 trips to the plate. Yastrzemski passed Cobb with 11,988, and Pete Rose became the all-time leader in 1982 and was still increasing his mark in 1985.

Aaron surpassed Cobb's 3,034 games played by appearing in 3,298 games during his 23-year career. Yastrzemski ended his career with 3,308 games played to pass Aaron but only to see Rose pass them all in 1984 as he finished that year with 3,371.

When Cobb's standards began falling as early as the 1930s, the so-called experts began shifting their stances. Records that could be broken by sheer longevity, such as number of games played and times at-bat, probably would be broken in time, but no one would ever break two of Cobb's marks. A man would have to play 21 years and average 200 hits a year to break Cobb's mark of 4,191 hits, and no one was ever going to hit for a lifetime average of .367 again.

When asked about those two records at a 1949 press conference prior to an old-timers game in New York, Cobb said, "They can have all the records they want except one. I'll always have the .367."

When a boy starts playing baseball, he doesn't think about breaking records, not realistically. When they grow up and become professional ballplayers, they only think about making it to the Majors. Established players in the twilight of their careers only think about hanging on with a Major League team. Only stars of the Game who are still regulars in the lineup after two decades of playing think about setting career records.

Pete didn't start thinking about breaking any lifetime marks until 1978 when he came within striking distance of Stan Musial's National League hits record. As he began breaking career records he started looking to see what was next and what was attainable. After Musial's mark of 3,630 and Aaron's 3,771 were behind him, he set his sights on Cobb's mark.

After the 1983 season, the Phillies told Pete he would be a part-time player and pinchhitter in 1984. No, said Pete. He wanted Cobb's record, and he was going to get it. If the Phillies didn't want him to get it in Philadelphia, he would find a team that wanted him to get it in their city. The Phillies had no alternative but to release Pete from his contract, and on October 19, 1983, they did just that.

Not many teams wanted Pete after the way he played in 1983. He would be 43 at the beginning of the 1984 campaign, and not many 43-year-olds could play every day and contribute as much as a 25-year-old.

But 25-year-olds aren't on the brink of setting a new record for hits in a career. General manager John McHale of the Montreal Expos recognized that fact, and he also realized that Montreal needed something to bolster the Canadian franchise's sagging attendance. He needed a crowd-pleaser, and Pete could fill the role better than anyone. Peter Edward Rose went north of the border for the 1984 campaign.

Dissension had become the trademark of the Expos. Dick Williams was fired as the manager in 1981, just before the end of the season, because some of his players were unhappy with him and their unhappiness was showing on the field. Jim Fanning came down from the front office and kicked the Expos into the playoffs but couldn't get them into the World Series. In 1982, Fanning's team finished third behind St. Louis and Philadelphia. Fanning went back to the front office for the 1983 campaign, and Bill Virdon took over as manager. Virdon couldn't improve on Fanning's third place finish, and the Expos record fell to 82-80.

McHale thought he knew what the problem was. His players didn't know *how* to win. Pete Rose did. McHale felt Pete could teach his new teammates how to be winners.

The problem wasn't as McHale thought. His players knew how to win; they just didn't seem to want to win. The Expos had power, speed, defense, hitting, and pitching. They had it all except one thing: teamwork. They had too many egos working for themselves instead of for the benefit of the team.

In '83, Al Oliver had been the firstbaseman. Pete Rose coming to Montreal meant he might have to share that duty with Pete, and Oliver was determined to make it to 3,000 hits in his career. Playing part-time would put a squeeze on that attempt. Warren Cromartie had been the rightfielder. Pete Rose might be put in left-field, which meant Tim Raines would have to be switched to right or center. If he went to center, then

Andre Dawson would have to be moved to right. Then there was Terry Francona who needed to play every day. Where did Cromartie fit in? And then there was catcher Gary Carter, the alleged team leader. How would he handle having a natural leader like Pete on the field every day?

McHale solved the problem of Oliver. He traded him to San Francisco. Cromartie removed himself to Japan to solve that situation. But Carter?

The Expos stumbled through the season under Virdon, and Pete didn't contribute the way he usually did. He couldn't; he was hurt. It was his right arm. He started the year in leftfield, but when he was injured he couldn't throw the ball well. He was forced to sit down for some games, only pinchhitting in a few others.

Every game Pete spent on the bench put Cobb's record further away instead of closer.

McHale woke up to reality as the year wore on and his team became less and less of a threat to the Cubs and Mets, the two teams that were setting the pace in the National League East. The Montreal fans weren't busting down the turnstiles to get into Olympic Stadium, and Pete's salary of $800,000 was beginning to drag on cash flow. When Bob Howsam asked him for permission to talk to Pete about managing the Reds, McHale was delighted.

Howsam wasn't exactly in love with Pete, but the Reds were in trouble. Manager Vern Rapp was killing the spirit of a young team, and after two straight last place finishes in the West, something had to be done to punch up the club's attendance. The Reds needed a drawing card, and Howsam knew the man for the job.

Pete said he would be delighted to return to Cincinnati but not as the manager. He had reached the 4,000 hit mark on April 13 with a double off Jerry Koosman of the Phillies at Olympic Stadium. He wanted 4,192 more than ever, and he couldn't get it unless he was playing.

Okay, okay. Howsam gave in. Pete could play if he also managed the Reds. Pete agreed, but only if he could have a guaranteed contract as a player that would carry him through the 1986 season. What could Howsam say? He said yes, and Pete Rose came back to his native city as the Reds' player-manager on August 16, 1984.

At that time, Pete was hitting .259 on 72 hits, giving him a career total of 4,062. He was 130 shy of the record he wanted so badly.

In 26 games with the Reds, Pete rapped out 35 more hits in 96 trips to give him an average of .365. Coming home put new life into his swing and new life into the club. Attendance went up and so did the Reds, climbing out of last place by going 19-23 with Pete at the helm. This gave Pete a winning percentage of .452 which was .060 higher than the Reds had been under Rapp. With Pete setting an example for them, many of the young players on the Reds responded by finishing the season on a promising note.

The Reds didn't make any earth-shaking trades over the winter. They had plenty of talented players. Some of them just needed experience, while others just needed to be led properly.

Before the 1985 season began, Pete determined that he would platoon himself at first base, the same as he had done the summer before when he took over as the Reds' manager. The question was who would platoon with him. Of course, he chose a younger man, his old friend, Tony Perez who was 42, a whole year younger than Pete. For second base he had Ron Oester, a veteran of five full seasons and a player many had called the new Pete Rose when he came up from the minors. For shortstop there was Tom Foley and ageless Davey Concepcion. Nick Esasky had been up and down at third, and Pete thought he saw enough in the power-hitting Esasky to platoon him with Wayne Krenchicki who had hit .298 the year before. The outfield would have Duane Walker and Eric Davis platooning in left; Eddie Milner and Gary Redus platooning in center; and veterans Dave Parker and Cesar Cedeno platooning in right. Pete's only problem position was at the catcher spot. None of the men who had played there the year before had shown much, and the group that came to spring training wasn't much better.

For pitching, Pete had Mario Soto, the strikeout artist with 77 career wins, 18 of them in '84. Soto would anchor an very young but otherwise promising staff. Jay Tibbs had gone 6-2 in 14 starts at the end of '84. Tom Browning had won one of his three starts in the final weeks of the previous campaign and had a fine ERA of 1.54 in 23-plus innings. John Franco was 6-2 out of the bullpen during his rookie season of '84. John Stuper was over from the Cardinals, and veterans Tom Hume, Frank Pastore, Ted Power, and Joe Price were around.

Dear Pete   **253**

On paper the 1985 Reds looked to be a lot better than the 70-92 team of 1984. On the field they began looking like the Reds of 1981, a team that had a 66-42 record in the strike-shortened season. If Pete could only find a catcher like Johnny Bench . . . hm-m-m.

As the season wore on and the Reds couldn't climb higher than 10 games over .500, new faces were added to the team. Cincinnati native Buddy Bell whose father Gus Bell had played for the Reds from 1953 through 1961 came over in a trade with the Texas Rangers. Bo Diaz was picked up in a trade with the Phillies. Max Venable was added for outfield depth.

As a player, Pete continued to platoon himself at first with Perez. Before the season began, Pete was asked when he thought he would break Cobb's record. Pete looked at a Reds' schedule and circled a date: Monday, August 26, the Reds would be home against the St. Louis Cardinals. Pete said it would be ideal because the game could be on national television.

One dark cloud blotted the otherwise blue skies of Baseball's summer. The Major League Players Association's contract with the owners had expired the winter before. A strike was a distinct possibility.

The MLPA turned their threat into a reality on August 6. The Players cleaned out their lockers and headed home. Commissioner Peter Ueberroth didn't stand aside as his predecessor had and let the two sides argue it out over the bargaining table. He stepped into the fray immediately, "for the good of Baseball." Within 48 hours Ueberroth had a peace treaty if not a full-fledged contract between the two parties, and the teams resumed play on the 8th. The games that were cancelled on the 6th and 7th were rescheduled.

As the Pete's predicted date approached, it became obvious that Pete would not break the record on the 26th. When that Monday came, Pete had 84 hits for the season, 11 short of breaking Cobb's 57-year-old record. At the rate he was going, it would be another two weeks before he was close enough to get it in one game.

The Reds finished their seven-game homestand on September 1, and Pete had 88 hits. The next six games would be on the road; three in St. Louis and three in Chicago against the Cubs, a team whose pitching staff had been decimated by injuries.

Beginning a week before, the Cubs' radio and television play-by-play announcers and color analysts kept telling listeners and viewers across the country that "Pete Rose and the Cincinnati Reds will be in town to play the Cubs next Friday, Saturday, and Sunday. He only needs..." And they would give the number of hits Pete needed to break Cobb's record.

Harry Caray, Dwayne Staats, Steve Stone, and Lou Boudreau, the Cubs media people, weren't the only ones touting Pete's progress. Hardly a day had gone by throughout the season that a story about Pete or a television interview with Pete didn't show up in print or on the tube, and as Pete came closer and closer to the record, the coverage grew and grew.

The Reds and Pete arrived in Chicago, and it looked like Pete wouldn't get a chance to tie the record, let alone break it, in the Windy City. Wrigley Field, Pete's favorite ballpark outside of Riverfront Stadium because it had natural grass and no lights which meant every game was played in daylight the way baseball was meant to be played according to Pete, would not add another historical event to its long list of great moments in the annals of Baseball. Manager Jim Frey of the Cubs had picked his probable starters for the three-game set before the Reds arrived. One of his choices was a lefty, Steve Trout, and another was a rookie pitcher, right-hander Derek Botelho, of whom Pete hadn't seen too much before. The third was veteran righty Dennis Eckersley who was coming back off an injury, so Frey only planned to let him throw 50 pitches, about four or five innings. That meant Pete would only start two games, and in one of those he would only get two, maybe three chances to see a pitcher he knew before being faced with relievers that he may never have hit against prior to that day.

In the first game, the wind was blowing out, and Pete got one up in the jetstream in the first inning for his 160th career homer. Much to his surprise, the Chicago fans called Pete out of the dugout and gave him a rousing ovation. Pete had been booed in Chicago ever since accidentally stepping on Ernie Banks' foot in 1969, some Chicago fans still blaming him for the Cubs demise in the late-going that year. Pete remarked about it during a post-game interview.

"You see those goat walks?" he said, pointing toward the "basket", a fence-like protrusion that hangs out over the playing field from the top of the outfield walls. "They put those in because of all the garbage the fans used to throw at me."

Later in the game, Pete got hit No. 4,189, a single off junk-balling righthander Reggie Patterson who was up from the minors for the tail-end of the season.

On Saturday, Eckersley looked good in his first start in over two months, keeping Pete off the basepaths his first two trips up. Rookie Jay Baller did likewise in the two times Pete faced him. Lee Smith walked Pete in the ninth, and that was that. He still had 4,189 hits.

Pete would be sitting out the final game of the series, so Reds' owner Marge Schott would get her wish of having Pete home in Cincinnati for the tying hit and the record-breaker. The San Diego Padres would be in town for four games starting Monday, September 9. Two of them would be make-up games; the two that had been cancelled by the very short players strike.

But a funny thing happened on the way to the park that Sunday, September 8. History gets changed by the oddest oddities, and the evening before Steve Trout fell off a bike and hurt himself, not seriously but enough for Frey to keep him out of lineup on Sunday. Just two hours before game time, the announcement was made that the Cubs would be starting Reggie Patterson. Pete immediately did the unexpected thing. He changed the lineup card to his lefthanded-hitting team, which included firstbaseman Pete Rose.

Just a few nights before in St. Louis, Pete didn't start against a Cardinal righthander, and some people wondered if he was holding back, purposely not playing just so he could tie and break the record in Cincinnati. Adding drama to his decision was the fact that his family, Carol and their son Ty, and Reds' owner Marge

Schott had returned to Cincinnati already and it was too late to call them back for the Sunday game. How would it be to tie and break Cobb's record without his wife and boss there to see him do it?

With mixed emotions, Pete stuck to his loyalty to his team. He had started against nearly every righthander all season long, so why change now? Let the hits fall where they may.

And hit he did. In the first inning, Pete dumped a single into centerfield. No. 4,190 was in the record books, providing the forecasted rain held off for five innings.

When the Reds were in the dugout for the top of the second, Dave Parker kept telling Pete not to do it, walking up and down repeating the same line, "Don't do it, don't do it." Davey Concepcion advised Pete to take his batting glove and go back in the clubhouse and watch the rest of the game on television. Pete ignored them both. He was a gamer, and this was a game.

After Pete rolled out to second in the third inning to drive in a run, Parker and Concepcion continued to advise him to take himself out. He owed it to the fans in Cincinnati to tie and break the record at home. Pete stayed in the game.

In the fifth inning, Patterson got two quick strikes on Pete, then missed the plate with the next three pitches to run the count full. Pete guessed fastball; Patterson came in with a screwball. It looked like a lame heater to Pete, so he swung *PR 4192*, the black bat made especially for him and his quest, and banged out hit No. 4,191.

The Chicago fans went wild. They gave the man his due.

Cubs' firstbaseman Leon Durham stood close to Pete during the ovation and said, "Don't move. I want to get some TV exposure." Pete looked over at the Cubs' dugout to see Steve Trout smiling broadly and gesturing toward himself with both hands. If not for some loose gravel, he would have started the game and Pete would have watched from the dugout still needing two hits to tie, three to break Cobb's record.

The weather had been a hot, humid 88° at game time. Not long after Pete tied Cobb's record, the skies grew dark and stormy. Pete came up in the seventh but failed to reach. Then the skies opened up, and the game was delayed for two hours.

Marge Schott had gone to the Seattle-Cincinnati opening game of the NFL season in Cincinnati that Sunday afternoon. She listened to the Reds game on a small portable radio, and when she heard Pete was in the lineup, she was frantic. All during the rain delay she tried to reach Pete by telephone but was unsuccessful.

After the game during the press session, Pete remarked, "I had 30,000 people yelling here, and one lady sitting back in Cincinnati kicking her dog every time I got a hit."

When the weather cleared, the Reds had one more chance to bat. So did Pete. He was scheduled to be the third man up in the ninth. The first two men reached off the Cubs' ace reliever, fireballer Lee Smith. The fastballs came in like aspirin tablets, and in the dim light of early evening, they looked even smaller to Pete. He struck out.

Back in the dugout, Pete's son Petey, who had come along on the road trip to St. Louis and Chicago, asked his dad, "Is it tough to see?"

Pete replied, "I don't know. It sounded like a strike, so I swung at it."

The game was halted after nine innings because of darkness, tied 5-5. The rule book states that a suspended game's statistics are not to be entered into the record books until the game is completed at a later date or called off because it cannot be rescheduled. The only exception to that is when the game in question is at Wrigley Field. Pete's two hits went into the record books for September 8, 1985.

The record was tied but not yet broken, and the Reds headed back to Cincinnati for a four-game set with the Padres. Both the Padres and the Reds were chasing the Dodgers in the NL West. They had taken turns being in second place for over a month, ever since the Dodgers had suddenly come to life in June and overtook both of them in July for first place. Each team needed to sweep the other if either had any hope of catching LA, the Dodgers having an 8½-game lead over the Reds that Monday morning.

San Diego manager Dick Williams had his rotation set for the series. Lefty Dave Dravecky would go in the first game, to be followed by Lamar Hoyt, Eric Show, and Andy Hawkins, all righthanders. The Cincinnati fans knew the rotation ahead of time, but still more than 29,000 of them, including this writer, showed up for the first game. At every opportunity, they chanted "We want Pete." But Pete stuck to the decision he had made in the spring. He used four pinchhitters during the game which the Reds won, 2-1, but he wasn't one of them.

Hoyt hadn't won a game in over a month, having missed a few turns with an injury. But in Game Two he was the pitcher the Padres hoped he would be. He got Pete out three straight times, and reliever Lance Mc-Cullers got him the last trip to the plate. A sell-out crowd went home disappointed, and I went back to my hotel room.

The daylight hours of September 11, 1985 dragged by for everyone with an interest in Pete getting hit No. 4,192. Evening finally came, and the lights went on at Riverfront Stadium. The players from both teams went through their usual warm-ups prior to the game: infield practice, batting practice, loosening up exercises, playing catch; everything routine. Then it was 7:30 p.m., the scheduled start of the game. But the fans were still pouring into the stadium. The game was held up more than a quarter of an hour in order to let as many people into the park as possible. Over 60,000 fans, many still looking for their seats or just good viewing room if they had purchased SRO tickets, crowded into the arena. By the time most of them reached their places, it was the bottom of the first inning.

Eric Vaughn Show of the San Diego Padres stood on the pitcher's mound as Peter Edward Rose, player-manager for the Cincinnati Reds, stepped into the batter's box. Up in the press box, the official scorer noted the time: 7:59.

Show got the signal from catcher Bruce Bochy. He

wound up and fired.

"Ball!" shouted the umpire on a high and outside pitch. Bochy threw the sphere back to Show, then crouched to give another signal. Show nodded, wound up again, and came with the second pitch.

Rose swung, but the ball sailed straight back to the screen. Foul, a strike. A new ball was put in play.

Bochy gave Show another sign. The pitcher's head bobbed in agreement, and he brought in another. Rose watched it all the way into the catcher's glove.

"Ball!" cried the ump. Good call. It was inside.

The count was now 2-1, a hitter's count. Show knew it; Rose knew it; Bochy knew it.

What to call? Bochy wondered.

What to throw? Show was thinking.

What's he coming with? Rose pondered.

It's a guessing game, and the question was who could outguess whom.

The time is 8:01 *post meridiem* Eastern Daylight Time, Wednesday, September 11, 1985, 57 years to the day since Ty Cobb had last come to bat as a Major League ballplayer. Eric Show went into his wind up to deliver a 2-1 pitch to the hitter. In came the ball, belt high, over the plate. The batter swung, making solid contact, and a liner screamed over the shortstop's head toward left-center. It dropped in no-man's land, bouncing so high off the synthetic turf that leftfielder Carmelo Martinez had to jump up to keep it from going over his head to the wall. Martinez hurried his throw into the shortstop as the batter rounded first.

Peter Edward Rose, the son of Harry "Pete" Rose

and his wife LaVerne, had achieved immortality by reaching base safely with the 4,192nd hit of his 23-year career as a Major League baseball player.

Pandemonium broke out at Riverfront Stadium. The throng stood and cheered and applauded. Fireworks exploded in the sky. The Reds' bench emptied onto the field as Pete's teammates congratulated him. The first to get to Pete was his long-time friend, Tommy Helms, who was coaching first base. Two more long-time friends, Tony Perez and Dave Concepcion, briefly hoisted him onto their shoulders. Eric Show, the pitcher who had served up the hit, came over and offered his congratulations. Petey Rose came out of the dugout, and his weeping father said to him, "I love you, and I hope you pass me." The ovation continued, and Pete wept on the shoulder of Tommy Helms.

And finally it was over, and the game resumed. Pete got another hit, a triple, hit No. 4,193, a new record made to be broken by Pete every time he gets another hit in an illustrious career that is still going on even as this book about him goes to press. How many hits will he have when he takes himself out of the lineup for the last time? Who knows?

The big knock, the hit that broke the record no one ever thought would be broken, was in the record books with the name of Pete Rose beside it.

The argument began the day Pete decided to break Ty Cobb's record. Does getting 4,192 hits make Pete Rose a greater ballplayer than Ty Cobb? How can this question ever be answered? Statistics are one measure of a player's career. How his teammates and opponents remember him is another. But does a player's personality have anything to do with his play? Does his life off the field have anything to do with his life on the field?

Ty Cobb was a fierce competitor. So is Pete. Cobb played and Pete still plays the game one way: to win; nothing else suffices. Cobb was feared, even hated by his opponents and teammates. Pete is respected and liked by his. Cobb played in one era of the game, and Pete is playing in another. A comparison between the two segments of Baseball history is impossible. Both times had their positives and negatives, and an honest discussion of them would take up another whole book.

And just like the eras in which they played, Pete Rose and Ty Cobb can't be compared. Each of them could be considered the greatest player of his time, but to say one of them is the greatest of all time can't be done.

Pete knows all about Ty Cobb's incredible career, and he, above all, appreciates the achievements of "The Georgia Peach".

And only Ty Cobb could truly appreciate the feats of Pete Rose. He never met Pete, and although Pete was a professional player before Cobb died in 1961, he probably never heard of him either. But Ty Cobb *knew* Pete.

The American Broadcasting Company interrupted their regularly televised program within seconds after Pete sliced hit No. 4,192 into left-centerfield to let America know that he had done the impossible. ABC showed the scene at Riverfront Stadium, first live after Pete was standing on first base, then replaying the hit. Besides the crowd's reaction other accolades began pouring in instantly. Among them were a telephone call to the stadium by President Ronald Reagan, a U.S. Senate resolution congratulating Pete on his accomplishment, and the renaming of Second Steet, the thoroughfare that runs by Riverfront Stadium, to Pete Rose Way by the Cincinnati city council.

More handshakes, pats on the back, and acknowledgements of his feat will come as time goes on, but the greatest of all these was given 30 years prior to Pete establishing a new career hits record.

The news department at ABC dug up a piece of old film which was shown at the end of their special bulletin about Pete's record. The subject of the film-clip was an interview of Ty Cobb. The interviewer asked Cobb what it would take to break his record of 4,191 hits in his career.

Cobb replied, "It would take a guy like me. A guy with real hustle."

Tyrus Raymond Cobb knew Peter Edward Rose.

20

Dear Pete

Men come and go, and some of them have their achievements etched in record books. Beyond the records there are contributions to mankind probably more significant than the records.

September 12, 1985

Dear Pete,

It's been over 23 years since I first heard your name. I was 16 then, and you were a rookie in the Reds' spring training camp. I was a Cub fan living in the California desert. So the only way I could follow Big League baseball was to listen to Vin Scully and Jerry Doggett do the Dodgers broadcast. That's how I heard your name the first time.

Scully was doing the play-by-play of a Reds-Dodgers exhibition when you came up to bat. His exact words are recorded somewhere, but here's my version of them:

"They tell me this kid Rose is a real hustler. He even runs out walks. He's only played three years in the minors. Last year he was at Macon in the Class A Sally League. With that limited

experience, he doesn't stand much of a chance of making the Majors this year, but watch out for him in the future. If hustle means anything, Pete Rose is going places in this Game."

I can't recall exactly how you hit that day, but the thing that still sticks in my mind is how Scully was impressed with hustle, your hustle especially.

When your name started showing up in the newspaper box scores that spring, I kept remembering Scully's words. When the Reds played the Dodgers, I listened to him rave about you some more, and I was that much more impressed myself.

I played high school ball, and that year I wanted to be a pitcher. I had a good fastball, no curve, and questionable control. When I missed my first opportunity to start a game due to illness and watched my replacement throw a two-hitter, I read the handwriting on the wall. If I was going to play that year, I'd better switch positions and quick. I asked the coach to put me in the outfield because I had a great arm and could get a good jump on anything hit my way. Before the week was out, I had hustled my way into the starting lineup and never let anyone push me out of it again. And believe me, that wasn't easy because we had guys who could run faster than me, hit better than me, throw better than me, and catch better than me. But no one could hustle better than me. Maybe I had that in me before then; I can't say for sure. But after I heard Scully say something about how you "attacked" the game, I figured that was the only way to play.

Dreams of making it to the Big Leagues began to grow in my head, but family circumstances, my own immaturity, a knee that had to have three operations in four years, and you changed the course of my life.

You won your first batting title the year the Navy put me on

Dear Pete 267

waivers. I was really happy for you, but I knew you'd earned it. By then I'd seen you play several times on TV, and I could tell you weren't as gifted as a lot of players. You got to the top on hustle and a desire to win. That set you apart, above the rest, even over my Cubs.

Over the next few years, I watched you become the complete superstar, and I kept trying to hustle my own life to some of the success you had achieved. I had a lot of set-backs. A daughter got very sick as an infant and almost died. If a long-time friend hadn't loaned me the money, I don't know how I would have paid the medical bills.

Shortly after that, I got a new job, one where hustle paid off. Up till then, I had jobs that had no future to them. I went to work in the circulation department of a daily newspaper in a large city. It was my responsibility to build and keep circulation in a certain part of the city. Immediately upon moving up from trainee to having my own district, I began putting the "Pete Rose Principle" to work. That's what I call taking the tools and talent you have, no matter how small and insignificant they may be, and you do everything in your power to make them work to get the best possible results. You see, I have always been a shy person, almost to the point of being timid, and I have difficulty meeting strangers. My job required me to meet a lot of strangers, but using the "PRP" got me through. The "PRP" made a winner out of me. Like you, I broke all the records, only I broke sales records, service records, and accounting records instead of batting records. The last time I visited some friends who still work for that newspaper was 1983, and my former supervisor told me that all of my records were still standing and no one had yet come close to them.

I changed jobs and let my limited success go to my head, and

*things started going downhill fast. It didn't take long to get back
to square one. Somehow I forgot the "PRP", and all the usual
emotional maladies hit me at once: depression, loss of self-
esteem, etc. I was on the verge of suicide.*

*Then I got the biggest break of my career a few years ago,
and without realizing it I applied the "PRP" to it. This break
suddenly reminded me of the admiration and respect I had for
you when I was a teenager, and upon reflection, I realized that
you had been a bigger influence on my life than I had given you
credit for.*

*My seventh grade teacher once quoted someone who said,
"A teacher never knows how far his influence will go." Whether
you know it or not, you're a teacher. You teach by example, by
your actions, by your results. You're no blowhard who says,
"You do it my way or hit the highway." No way. You go out and
you do it. You show people how it's done by doing it.*

*I could go on and on praising you for your accomplishments
on the baseball field, but that's not the purpose of this letter. I'm
writing to thank you for being you. It wouldn't make any
difference if you weren't a baseball player. You could be a
doctor, a pipefitter, a cowboy, whatever. I know a lot of people
who are like you. They are good at what they do because they
try to be the best they can be, just like you. You have always
tried to be the best you can be, and that's what makes you
great, not all the numbers in the record books. Those records
would be pretty shallow if they were accomplished by an
athlete who had all the talent in the world but only used half of
it. Your records take on special meaning because you worked
your tail off to get them.*

*I've read a lot about you this past year or so, and I was most
impressed by what I read about your relationship with your*

Dear Pete   **269**

*father and your relationships with your children. My dad and I
weren't close like you and your dad. I envy you that. But I've got
a chance yet to be close to my children the way you are with
yours. I hope my kids all turn out like you. They don't have to be
baseball greats. I just want them to be the best that they can be,
like you, no matter what they choose to do in life.*

*I know I'm not alone when I say once again, "Thanks, Pete,
for being you."*

Your humble admirer,

L———

Very few people exercise an influence on society
during their lifetimes. I could name a whole list of men
and women who have affected people in some positive
way, but there's no need for that. Let me just say that I
would place the name of Pete Rose on that list.

Pete's fans are his admirers, and he has justified their
admiration and respect with his personal integrity,
dedication, and hustle.

Thank you, Pete, from all of us.

Pete Rose's Regular Season Statistics

YEAR	G	AB	R	H	D	T	HR	RBI	SB	AVE
CINCINNATI										
1963	157	623	101	170	25	9	6	41	13	.273
1964	136	516	64	139	13	2	4	34	4	.269
1965	162	670	117	209	35	11	11	81	8	.312
1966	156	654	97	205	38	5	16	70	4	.313
1967	148	585	86	176	32	8	12	76	11	.301
1968	149	626	94	210	42	6	10	49	3	.335
1969	156	627	120	218	33	11	16	82	7	.348
1970	159	649	120	205	37	9	15	52	12	.316
1971	160	632	86	192	27	4	13	44	13	.304
1972	154	645	107	198	31	11	6	57	10	.307
1973	160	680	115	230	36	8	5	64	10	.338
1974	163	652	110	185	45	7	3	51	2	.284
1975	162	662	112	210	47	4	7	74	0	.317
1976	162	665	130	215	42	6	10	63	9	.323
1977	162	655	95	204	38	7	9	64	16	.311
1978	159	655	103	198	51	3	7	52	13	.302
PHILADELPHIA										
1979	163	628	90	208	40	5	4	59	20	.331
1980	162	655	95	185	41	1	1	64	12	.282
1981	107	431	73	140	18	5	0	33	4	.325
1982	162	634	80	172	25	4	3	54	8	.271
1983	151	493	52	121	14	3	0	45	7	.245
MONTREAL-CINCINNATI										
1984	121	374	43	107	15	2	0	34	1	.286
CINCINNATI										
985*	105	360	52	96	12	2	2	42	0	.267
TOTALS	3476	13771	2142	4193	738	133	160	1285	187	.305

* Thru September 11, 1985

Dear Pete   **271**

INDEX

Dear Pete

Dear Pete

O'TOOLE, Jim — 77
OTT, Mel — 81
OWENS, Paul — 240, 242

P

PAFKO, Andy — 82
PALMER, Jim — 159, 184
PARKER, Dave — 253, 259
PARKER, Harry — 197
PASTORE, Frank — 253
PATTERSON, Reggie — 257, 258
PAVLETICH, Don — 77
PEREZ, Tony — 33, 38, 41, 61, 142, 152,
   157, 160, 183, 185, 186, 188, 190, 197,
   199, 202, 205, 206, 209, 223, 225, 242,
   253, 254, 263
PERRANOSKI, RON — 92
PIERSALL, Jimmy — 20, 233
PINSON, Vada — 77, 78, 86, 106, 111, 147
PLUMMER, Bill — 38, 54
POST, Wally — 68, 149
POWELL, Boog — 184
POWER, Ted — 253
PRICE, Joe — 253
PURKEY, Bob — 77

Q

QUEEN, Mel — 66, 141
QUISENBERRY, Dan — 231, 232

R

RAINES, Tim — 250
RAPP, Vern — 251, 252
RAYE, Martha — 136
REAGAN, Ronald — 265
REARDON, Jeff — 238
REDFORD, Robert — 11
REDUS, Gary — 253
REED, Ron — 240
RETTENMUND, Merv — 199
REYES, Nat — 63
RICE, Jim — 203
RICKEY, Branch — 223
RIVERS, Mickey — 33
ROBERTS, Dave — 224
ROBERTSON, Bob — 185
ROBINSON, Brooks — 184
ROBINSON, Frank — 77, 78, 79, 106, 112,
   149, 184, 248
ROBINSON, Jackie — 176
ROGERS, Steve — 224, 238
ROSE, Carol — 257
ROSE, Caryle — 16
ROSE, Dave — 13
ROSE, Fawn — 57
ROSE, Harry (Pete) - 12, 13, 17, 18, 21, 50,
   59, 62, 78, 161, 262
ROSE, Jackie — 16
ROSE, Karolyn — 38, 54, 105, 153, 160,

210, 234
ROSE, LaVerne — 12, 263
ROSE, Lois — 16
ROSE, Peter, Jr. (Googie, Petey, Petie) —
   57, 160, 260, 263
ROSE, Tyler Edward (Smoogie) — 57, 257
RUDI, Joe — 188, 201
RUDUSELL, Ken — 15
RUIZ, Chico — 183
RUSSELL, Billy — 199
RUTH, Babe — 83, 87, 126, 247
RUTHVEN, Dick — 229, 230
RYAN, Mike — 91
RYAN, Nolan — 140, 230, 236

S

SADECKI, Ray — 143
SANDBERG, Ryne — 240
SANGUILLEN, Manny — 187
SCHEINBLUM, Richie — 192
SCHMIDT, Mike — 226, 228, 232, 240
SCHOTT, Marge — 257, 258, 259
SCULLY, Vin — 266
SEAVER, Tom — 140, 194, 197
SEGHI, Phil — 59, 60
SEGUI, Diego — 203
SELMA, Dick — 144
SHAW, George Bernard — 234
SHOW, Eric — 260, 261, 262, 263
SIMPSON, Wayne — 152, 183, 184, 192
SIMS, Duke — 158
SISLER, Dick — 111
SKINNER, Bob — 80
SLAUGHTER, Enos — 69
SMITH, Lee — 257, 259
SMITH, Lonnie — 229, 240
SMITH, Ozzie — 240
SOTO, Mario — 253
SOUEL, Larry — 61
SPAHN, Warren — 82, 92
SPENCER, Daryl — 77, 89
STAATS, Dwayne — 255
STANLEY, Mickey — 138
STARGELL, Willie — 187, 228
STAUB, Rusty — 194
STEINBECK, Bobby — 65
STEINBRENNER, George — 208, 239
STENGEL, Casey — 182
STONE, George — 197
STONE, Steve — 255
STOWE, Bernie — 211
STUPER, John — 241, 253
SUTTON, Don — 201, 222
SWAN, Craig — 225

T

TEMPLE, Johnny — 149
TEMPLETON, Gary — 227, 237
TENACE, Gene — 189, 190, 191
THOMSON, Bobby — 81, 194

Dear Pete